Poetry of Kamala Das
The Aesthetic Dimension

Poetry of Kamala Das
The Aesthetic Dimension

Dinesh K. Shukla

ADHYAYAN

ADHYAYAN PUBLISHERS & DISTRIBUTORS
New Delhi-110002

Published by
ADHYAYAN PUBLISHERS & DISTRIBUTORS
4378/4B, 105, J.M.D. House, Murari Lal Street
Ansari Road Darya Ganj, New Delhi - 110002
Ph.: 011-23263018, 011-23277156, Fax: 23280028
Email: adhyayanpublishers@yahoo.com

Poetry of Kamla Das
The Aesthetic Dimension

Edition 2010
ISBN 978-81-8435-245-0

Printed in India

Published by Harish Chandra Yadav for Adhyayan Publishers & Distributors, Delhi. Laser Typesetting at Jain Computers and Printed at Tarun Offset Printers. Delhi

Dedicated

To

Universal Motherhood which makes our life living

Foreword

Indian English Poetry does not have much to cheer about after the era of Sri Aurobindo and Tagore was over. While the Indian English Novel had seen the great trio of Anand-Narayan-Raja Rao, poetry still needed a major figure who could inaugurate an era or establish a canon. This was particularly so about the Indian English Women's poetry where Sarojini Naidu and Dutt sisters wrote pretty elegant poetry which had a significant impact upon the nationalist movement as well as national sensibility, but a voice which could define what Indian English Women's poetry couldbe like was almost missing. It is in this connection that the poetry of Kamala Das is so important to us. She changes the idiom, expression, imagery and the view about women held for centuries as sancrosanct and religiously pious.

Susie Tharu and Lalitha did quite a job by editing the two volume anthology on Indian English Women's writing. However, the volumes leave much to be desired. They begin fairly late in the history of a nation whose literature goes back to more than five thousand years. Geneaological and chronological burdens do tell their own tale and they can neither be discredited nor sidelined. Indian society was largely permissive during much of its historical evolution before the invasion of India by the Muslims. We have distinguished women philosophers in the *Upanishads, Smritis* and the rest. Vedic seers adored Nature as mother. *Rig Vedic* hymns on the Savitur, Indra, Mithra, Varun, Ushas are all addressed to the powers of nature which has been allegorised. Woman is already a metaphor in terms of the language of literature, but here she is raised to the status of a goodess who can diversify at will, multiply, and grant boons to her devotees for the common benefit of human society. This view, now considered to be highly idealistic, was in practice indeed during that time. Hence the famous Sanskrit saying: *yatra naryasa pujyante ramante tatra devata* – where women are warshipped, there the gods live. The stories of Shakuntala and Dushyant, and before them, Yayati and Devyani-Sharmistha speak volumes of the permissiveness of the Indian society, its mobility freedom and openness. Women were no disjunctural points of blockages to the evolving discourse abut humanity. They constituted an integral part of it. Except for Brahmputra river, the rest of the Indian rivers are named after women and worshipped as goddesses. India had no nature/culture dichatomy as it wa in the West. *Prakriti* and *Purusha* have been an inalienable part of Indian consciousness and the two cannot be imagined to be apart from each other.

Vatsayan's *Kam Sutra,* considered to be the fifth *Veda,* climaxes or even radicalises the study of women by linking each of her body parts of a cosmology of its own. Woman's body becomes a means to self-realization and the realisation of God. We speak of Sita-Ram, Radhey Shyam where female consorts come first and men later. The sculputure at Khajuraho speaks volumes of what woman's body has meant to India and Indians. It is a spiritual possession of mankind which gives us an epistemic field out of which grow*Mimansa, Nyaya, Vedanta, Samkhya* and the rest of the Schools of Indian philosophy. In the *aagam* and *nigam* traditions of the Indian scriptural consciousness, women have occupied a very high place in the hierarchies of gods and goddesses. However, the good work of the earlier tradition is almost put to waste by certain texts of the *Smriti* tradition like the *Manusmriti* which considers women as a commodity for consumption. The division of Indian society into castes and sub-castes served to inflame the dichotomous fires which reduced women to the margins of an (un)civil society. Buddhism, Sikkhism,

Jainism tried to reform the diseased society and were also successful to a large extent in their own times.

In the *tantric* traditions, women are considered to be *bhairavie* — a name generally given to Parvati, the wife of Lord Shiva. The secret of the founding of the relationships has been the paradigm of gods and goddesses that percolates down the human beings. This is so because they are also given the freedom and the choice to rise to the level of gods and goddesses who they worship to begin with. A culture so wide open in its epistemic doors and so deep in its ontological premises could not be charged with committing atrocities on women against which the likes of Kamala Das have to revolt. But strange as it may seem, Indian society underwent a lot of negative changes during and after the Muslim invasion. Our transitions of classical and folk music, our forms of architecture, man-woman relationship all underwent a redical change and Indianness came to be understood and defined in a new way altogether now. Formerly, *rasa* or the essence element was at the core of all human relationship particularly that between man and woman. The advant of this British did no good as wrong kind of values got polarised and the march towards the commercialization of the commodity called women was laid open. Because of the barbarities of culture that certain invaders brought with them, the position of women in India became more horrible than was imaginable at one point of time. Women became museum pieces within the household limits and a patriarchal system did the rest of the damage. It seemed time had come to a standstill and it may take millenniums before things mend.

Indian sensibility has a remarkable capacity to bouce back. When India was fighting its freedom struggle against the British, women generated all kinds of resistances and competently served as the second line of defense, the names of the likes of Laxmi Bai standing apart. It will not be unfair to say that what Laxmi Bai did for India's freedom struggle, Kamala Das has done for reconstituting the concept of Indian womanhood. Both are radical in their strategies and redefine paradigms in decadent times. The rise of the French women liberation movement has had quite as impact on the countries where English has served either as mother tongue or used as a second language. Because of the largeness of the historical continuum that India has seen, this movement did not effect Indian women to the extent it was expected. This was so because of the different set of problems Indian women encountered and the model offered to them carried its own brand inadequacies. The immediate predecessor of Kamala Das was Sri Aurobindo whose *magnum opus, Savitri* presented the idealistic tale of a woman who vntures to go to the Lord of Death in order ta bring back her dead husband. Kamala Das revolted against such idealistic presentations of women and opted far a realist and representationalist view which carried along with itself a certain linearity and corporeality of vision. This view was unfazed and undaunted by social pressures, challange as it did the conservative set-up of the Indian society.

Simone de Beauvoir's classic *The Second Sex* inaugurated a debate about women that is still continuing. Helen Cioux, Chodorov, Kate, Millet, Jullia Kristeva, Toril Moi, Patricia Spacks are some of the leading theorist writing on women. Elaine Showalter has taken an integralist view and cansiders women's literary criticism in the wilderness for women do not know what do they want. A female language as distinct from a male remains a dream and the issues are mugged up as well. Biological, linguistic, psycho-analytic and cultural are the four models under which Showalter tries to understand woman's prablems. There are practioners of all these models as well. The hallmark of all these models is the exposition of the binary according to which man is the architect of all crimes against women and as long as he survives in the system, women have little hope of getting redeemed. To the extent the argument goes, it works well. But it falls upon its own ground since all women begotten by a mother have still male inseminations. The cry for a distinct fmale experience gets murkier since many a male respond like females and *vice versa.* The concept of *ardhanarishwara* is not within the perceptual limits of Western feminism since that culture is biased and prejudiced against all normativities that go beyond the empirical realm. Transcendentalism is now treated as part of the politics man has been playing against woman's body and interests. Women are representational characters which apparently they are but to stop at that is to practise a fallacy. This fallacy is the *aporia* of Western feminism. As long as transcendental signifiers will be taken as part of the social schemata to pulvarize women and put them at the back doors of development, women will not be liberated. Western feminism grounds feminity in a certain kind of materialism which is unbecoming of itself given the Indian context. From the margin to the centre is a substantial cry and women are achieving milestones day in and day out. However, the question remains: Is that what being a woman means? Buddha's Fire Sermon has been put up side down. The body is lit up with passions, forms of possessivenesses and the will to power. Kamala Das is celebrating this fire; she would not read enough of Hindu scriptures, in spite of being born as a brahmin, that will add a metaphysical dimension to her poetry. She celebrates wild energies and is thirsty for them. *ABC of Lust* is a welcome addition to the orientational modes of Indian novel in English by women but it is decidedly belittling oneself. Women are trying to establish the variety of *maya,* illusion, a concept which Adi Shankaracharya gave while expounding the *Brahm Sutras.*

It is very much understable that a creative writer, particularly a female, has to make all sorts of adjustments if she has to continue to be a writer. Dinesh K. Shukla has done well to highlight psychological tensions that Kamala Das underwent while keeping alive her expressive component. Kamala Das believes in the exposition of her body for the figure is more important than any discussion about it. Man cannot boast of a body like that of a woman which is tender and strong at the same time, beautiful and lusty, ideational and real, living the binaries of life more successfully than man. Aesthetics of Kamala Das's poetry is born out of her body, her instincts, her possions, her lust which she unhinderingly has for men. It is a new kind of woman born in Indian contexts—a renaissance curvature of history which borders on *Gita's* statement given by Krishna that Nature in itself is wayward, boisterous and chaotic; in a minute it shall destroy the world if I do not control it by my will power. But Kamala Das is revolting precisely against such male chauvanism which is the will to dominate. Instinct for beauty and aesthetics are not always supported by society. Kamala Das is not searching for a Krishna as Meera did for that would be banality. She would also not like to be a *sati* Savitri which is a misnomer and an absurd impossibility. She would like to live her existence in flesh and blood, loving a man who could also have the same kind of passion and sexual urgency that she has for that man. Since Kamala Das did not get one in her life, she changed religion, husbands but the quest remained unfulfilled. Instead of getting immersed into the sea of love, she lands herself on a barren island where the realities she aspired for during her life time become bounds running wildly after her in order to finish off her existence. This is quite paradoxical but this is how it is. Dinesh successfully brings out her tensional aesthetics and the cry for beauty which remains more a hunger than a form of fulfilment. Dinesh's selection of the poems is handy to the theme and Kamala Das's kind of radical feminism is well exposed and interpreted by the author. Secret narratives of the body are over when one arrives at Kamala Das. Shame belongs to the system and not to her. Beauty is not a stigma but a statement. Whatever the pitfalls of her radical feminist model, the poetry of Kamala Das has created a new kind of space in Indian English poetic tradition specially in terms of the promiscuity of language, the passion and the warmth that it generates is almost unprecented. She is no mystic to the end of her life and her communions do not seek spiritual fulfiment which there is none. In a biological model, woman's body itself is the text; the text has the capacity to generate its own kind of illusions because it can multiply itself by begetting children. There is no castration complex since penis, which Freud called the fountain pen, cannot do any thing on its own; it needs a writing pad which is what woman's body is all about. But Kamala Das is not subscribing to any theoretical system; She is advancing woman's body itself as a role model which can work wonders and change woman's conditions. She does revolt against patriarchy but does not seem to uphold matriarchy to any appreciable degree. Her position is a curious in-between who is willing to go either side given the bodily and mental satisfaction it demands. Kamala Das's poetry is *jouissance* poetry a poetry of rhythm and energy, gyrating body compartments which have four thousand volts of electric current that will go waste if not properly lighted. Dinesh has done well to bring forth such ambivalences that one perceives in any aesthetic consideration of her poetry. I commend the author for having done a good work within limitations that Kamala Das's poetry imposes and releases at the same time. This is, perhaps, the core argument of the aesthetics of the poetry.

Charu Sheel Singh

Preface

Kamala Das Surraiya (b.1935-2009) emerged as first line feminist author of the post-1950 poetry scene of India. During her childhood days she was known as Madhavikutty a typical Keralite name. She was born in Kerala in an orthodox, and conservative Nair Brahmin family where her grandmother and mother used to compose Bhakti poems in mother tongue Malayalam. The literary atmosphere of Kamala Das's family helped her to incline towards poetry in an early age. She composed good and promising poetry not exactly in the style and content of grandmother and mother; she showed by her early compositions the element of revolt against and disagreement from orthodox and conservative atmosphere of parental home. Like any other daughter Kamala Das was trained to follow family norms, but after having seen dire consequences of mismatched relation of parents, she dedicated her entire creative energy in the study of wailing women's life.

To keep Kamala Das aloof from dirty social surrounding, parents arranged her education at home. However, Kamala Das's poetic vision could reach the most veiled aspects of woman's life. Her mission of literature has been to liberate woman from every kind of exploitation, orthodoxy, authoritism and injustice. Her iconoclastic personality launched a war first of all tendering advices against father's feudal and exploitative temperament. A young daughter's warring stance was no way tolerable to conservative father hence she was declared as "a defaming daughter." The ideological rift that developed between father and daughter kept increasing until the last breath of father. Kamala Das's pro-Feminist stance was to encounter more and more injustices targeted towards women in different garbs. Not only parental authority was challenge to Kamala Das rather political and religious authorities were also creating tough challenge to her.

I consider that to Kamala Das her poems were the tool of war and purification of gendered mind and society. She has composed three volumes of poetry, and a novel in English which all have been studied. Her writings in Malayalam have not been included in this study. The poems are studied with a specific purpose to trace out aesthetic elements which other available scholarships have generally ignored. I humbly offer this work for fond readers of feminism and students to make impartial and objective assessment.

This project could not have been a reality without financial assistance of UGC, for which I tender my cordial thanks to the same. I visited, Kerala Sahitya Academy library Trissur, Research Library B.H.U. Varanasi, British Council Library, New Delhi, respectable members of these libraries provided materials which I needed in the completion of this work. They all deserve special mention.

To Prof. Charu Sheel Singh Department. of English. Kashividyapith Varanasi I offer cordial gratitude for taking keen interest in the job. My parents have considerable share in making the project a success by the way of unconditional blessing which I do admit wholeheartedly. My wife Smt. Pramila Shukla, son Shreesh and daughter Jaya have influenced my work in curious ways I, therefore, recall them all dearly. The 'wild and anarchic' energy for justice and democracy that Dr. Rajeev Singh Kanoujia, reader Department. of Pol. Science has have influenced me deeply, hence I recall him with due love. To Bhuwan Tiwari I express my gratitude for advices he tendered. Last but not the least Prof. J.C. Tiwari, H.O.D. English and Dr. Poornima Bhatnagar reader in English Govt. PG College Ramnagar deserve their share of thanks. I hope this book to be equally useful to skilled readers of feminist poetry and university students preparing for their UG / PG degrees. Discrepancies if any belong to me, and usefulness to my well-wishers.

Dinesh K. Shukla

Place - Ramnagar
Nainital

Contents

1

Kamala Das and Her Age

Kamala Das (1935–2009) was born at Ernakulam, Kerala in a conservative Brahman Nayar family. She was privately educated, and afterwards developed as a bilingual writer of poetry and fiction in English and mother tongue Malyalam. Kamala Das has published three books of verse in English: *Summer in Calcutta* (1965). The *Descendants* (1967) *The Old Playhouse and Other Poems* (1973) and a novel *The Alphabet of Lust*. The time Kamala Das started her creative career was just after the independence of India. Indian people at large were in a state of romantic extravaganza which was shattered soon by confronting the hard realities of life. The absurd political promises proved futile and short lived. Indian youth were met with frustration and despair because of un-connectivity between governmental agencies and common man. The colonial sentiment of rich and affluent people has yet not gone off. They even after independence treated working people with hatred and considered them still colonized. The social and domestic condition of average Indian women was like a colony under a colony. They were bound to tolerate the pains of domestic and social marginalization. Despite laying, down their life for family and society under different roles they never got proper due of thanks and honour. Different institutions operating under customary and constitutional ambit had no space secured for better halves. They were thrown to backstage where neither ray of knowledge reaches nor money showers. Women society in general was out from mainstream nationalism consequently their confidence level was zero against their counterparts.

In such a time of emotional and confidential bankruptcy a host of feminist writers emerged on the literary surface of India, of these writers Kamala Das can be understood as flag bearing and path breaking pioneer. What Mary Erulkar has said about Kamala Das is correct in many respect. She said Kamala Das did "the bitter service to woman hood."[1] Her writing and life-style have been certainly awesome and furious for conservative social and domestic network of India. Her poetry and fiction have frank, open and uncommon discripton which does not suit Indian context, as M.K. Naik studies Kamala Das's writing, "The most obvious (and to the casual reader colourful) feature of Kamala Das's poetry is the uninhibited frankness with which she talks about sex, referring nonchalantly to the musk of sweat between the breast, 'the warm shock of mestrual blood' and even my pubis" [2] Such kind of description of private feminine organs in Indian orthodox society is an invitation to calamity as far as woman author is concerned. Scrutiny of her writing reveals what and why she has written is not out of place and relevance. Like any other woman Kamala Das has always been searching for love which she never found except despair and dejection. The personal life of Kamala Das after marriage was devastated because of her attitude always clashing with husband's.

She never diluted her identity from an individual to a 'flesh' which husband wanted, that ego conflict resulted into fiasco. Her cult of roubstism was not unwarranted rather a revolt against systemic negligence she met with and yearning for individuality prompted her to write the way she wrote. Despite defiance to patriarchy Kamala Das is a simple and domestic woman the fact remained concealed behind the stormy surface of her life. Her search for balance in conjugal proximity is objectified by the myth of Radha-Krishna as an ideal love parameter.

She has manifested many faces of woman according to roles assigned to them by social obligations. "Several faces of Eve are exhibited here-woman as sweetheart flirt, wife, woman of world, mother, middle aged matron. ...."[3] These conditional role-masks change but at centre a basic woman remains the same who is least loved but most betrayed object. All her life Kamala Das has been fighting against the tendency of betrayal rampant in the patriarchy. Along with Kamala Das there have been many woman writers advocating feminist cause in their respective style.

Monika Verma (1961) has six volumes to her credit: *Dragon Flies, Draw Flames* (1962), *Past Imperative,* (1972) *Alaknanda* (1976) to mention a few major works. She has translation of *Geet Govind* to her credit also. Her response to nature is very tender and mind-catching. Her feminist concern is not that much acute as Kamala Das's. She has honour for past manners but seems much bended towards future moderations in the life style of new age women.

Gauri Desh Pandey enjoys tremendous popularity as a feminist poet. She has three poetry collections: *Between Births* (1968), *Lost Love* (1970) and *Beyond the Slaughter House* (1972) has by and large open hearted welcome to the changing temperament of nature and society. She creates "the drama of man-woman relationship as evocatively as Kamala Das though on a much more limited scale and ina less challenging manner."[4] Gauri Desh Pandey seems unsatisfied with what has been happening to Indian woman in their socio-domestic sphere but her criticism is not that much penchant as of Kamala Das's. Her some lyrics are prone to tear and sigh by offering gloomy surroundings of their protagonist.

Mamta Kalia (1942) a bilingual author has so far only one collection of English verse, *Tribute to Papa* (1970) and many verse volumes in Hindi. She talks about love, marriage, family, and social and psychological problems coming up in the already entangled life of Indian woman.

Mamta Kalia having been a teacher and principal in a

girls college for 'long time has better sympathy to and understanding of adolescent girls' physical and mental changes. By the end of her creative career the force of her voice was a bit softened and became compromising. Kamala Das on the other hand never showed any sign of surrender and dilution of her avowed standpoint. Her war against normative pattern of relationship and life-style stood aflamed till date of death. Sunitinam Joshi wrote (1941), *Cyclone in Pakistan* (1971) and *Jackass and the Lady* (1980). The echoes and phrasal patches of Sarojini Naidu can be abundantly found in Sunitinam Joshi's poems. Her maturer work *Myth in a Mirror* contains poems on feminist psychology and mental conflict often aggravated because of circumstantial pullings. It has obtained a mythical character in the life of average Indian woman.

Tilottama Rajan though yet in progress makes bold experiments "with both verse inspired by painting and modern sculpture and typographical effects"[5] largerly in the tradition of Keats and Yeats. However, her achievement as an independent powerful feminist voice has not yet found requisite pitch that could register a group of loving readers.

Margaret Mukherji is another emerging and catching name in feminist writing who taught philosophy and has some nice collections of poetry to her credit. *The Spring and the Spectacle* (1967) is first collection saturated with personal and trained feminist note. Another author of that tradition is Tapati Mukherji whose *Golden Road to Smarkand* (1967) has been read widely with a note of applaud. A poetry collection *Theri Gatha* is composed under Budhist impact showing her bending towards deeper philosophical matter. Rosehn Alkaji's *Seventeen Poems* (1965) is remarkable set of poems for British style of phrasing because of her schooling in England. Sujata Bala Subramaniam's way of composing poetry is a kind of assurance to the readers about bringht future of Indian poetry in English. She operates upon phrases and emotions like a surgeon as per the need of the subject and the readers. Apart from these names there are still many coming up only to name a few: Shasthi Brata, Leela Dharamraj, Mary Erulkar,

M.C, Gabriel, Paul Jacob, S. Santhi, Sukanta Chaudhury. This chain of poets is in excellent making that can go pretty long, however they have shown distinct features of their works only in one or two collections that have lured the reader's attention.

English poetry written by feminist writers after 1950 has distinct quality of being assertive and unconventional in theme and style mainly imbibing contemporary subjects. P. Lal founder member of *Writers Workshop* in Calcutta has expressed his views and reservations about writing in Indian Engilsh and native dialect:

> Without trying to be facetious I should like to suggest that only in English can real Indian poetry be written; any other poetry is likely to be Bengali- slanted or Gujrati-biased and so on. Only Indian writing in English can hope to attain the Indian flavour. I cannot imagine a Punjabi writing Bengali poetry or Maharastriyan wring Hindi poetry but there are Tamilians, Bengalis, Punjabis, Gujratis, Jews, Goan, Sikkimise - all Indians writing in English on Indian themes or for Indian readers.[6]

English, according to P. Lal is not only a language of expression of 'Indianness' but a thread of national unity admitted and practiced by authors of new generation. During a long process of English application at various levels, most significantly in creative exercises by authors of Indian origin it has been Indianized in matters of syntax, sentence formation, idioms and diction. There is a lot of Indian impact on English which no author or linguist can deny. The post colonial wave drastically answered to an Eurocentric doctrination of English language. English having been in practice of colonial countries as a language of creativity and contact has taken shape of almost native dialect such as American, Canadian, Indian, Africa, Australian and Latin American English. These global units have donated to and were benefited by English through different activities. Thus feasibility and flexibility of English was increased by practicing countries.

The importance of English as a global mode of interaction has been accepted by Kamala Das in a promising poem "An Introduction:

> I am Indian, very brown, born in
> Malabar, I speak three languages write in
> Two, dream in one. Do not write in English they said
> English is not your mother tongue.

These assertive statements of Kamala Das put her ahead to others not in the matter of language but in other subjects too. Writing poetry for Kamala Das is a journey to exteriority and interiority altogether a Charu Sheel Singh a poet and theorist critic of world repute has also admitted in an interview to N.R. Gopal regarding his style of poetic composition that applies to all genuine poetry no matter what its subject-matters are:

> I do not choose my themes, themes come to me as a forms of destiny and carry their own destination. ....For me poet is a creatively passive person who has enough space within himself to let the forms enter into his body and allow his mind to frame appropriate stylistic pattern............[7]

The entire interview of Charu Sheel Singh focuses on an unknown process of creation that highlights passivity of the poet creatively engaged. Kamala Das unlike Charu Sheel Singh is passive towards her subject-matters hoping them to come to her, rather she approaches them effortedly because of her missionary zeal. Kamala Das is an individualistic and aggressive poet having poetry in her blood as her mother and grandmother had been poets in Malayalam. Her poems initially appeared in P.E.N. and other magazines of the time before the independent publication of *Summer in Calcutta.* Kamala Das explored in these collections different situations of city bred life in concrete and symbolic manner. About content and style of *Summer in Calcutta* Srinivas Iyenger comments, "under the Indian Sun, although sensuality lures, irristibly yet it fails to satisfy, feeling and introspection but sounds the depths of oceanic sense of frustration, and the calm of fulfillment eludes for ever."[8]

Kamala Das's manner in approaching the subject-matter is marked with leopard like adroitness that reveals her internal texture of personality. She is always on mission of battle that she as a typical Indian woman is destined to be engaged for her dejected community. The surrounding circumstances of Indian women are tough to alter and still tougher is to bring out aesthetic elements there from. This kind of mamath task Kamala Das has undertaken under the load of which she sometimes feels fragmented and sometimes unified; the personal mood of Kamala Das gets reflected in the phrases and emotions manifest in the poems as Srinivas Iyengar also remarked. "Her characteristic trick is to split phrases and meaning, even the infinitives, between two lines and this is surely symbolic of the fissured, or fractured sensibility she wishes to communicate."[9]

Kamala Das wishes to communicate her sentiments and harsh realities of women's life which they are bound to undergo unavoidably. A kind of confinement of body and soul is the life for women since birth till death. All their sacrifices and dedications to social and familial authorities are declared null and void and go unmentioned. In this way their life by and large is no life but a heap of nothingness whose existence is unnoticed by kith and kins. As a warrior of feminist battle Kamala Das not only wants to win but make winning a eternal phenomenon. Her battle of existence and identity is not motivated by false principle of superiority but, by quest of equality, love and mutuality. On the ground of entire poetic output of Kamala Das and opinions of scholars and critics of her poetry and fiction, are valid and substantial certificate to declare that Kamala Das is not only a feminist poet but much more. She prepares a highway of aesthetics by ingredients like love, compassion, and mutual understanding achieved by long battle against patriarchal mindset not for women only but for those too who promises adherence to these noble qualities.

The period of sixties in Indian history is marked with ideological clash between Gandhian and Nehruvian approach to humanity. After transfer of power from white Christian rulers to black Indian rulers has divided Indian society into two apparent blocks. Gandhian ideology which enthused freedom - fighters against alien rule was strategically sidelined the very day Nehru succeeded the crown of India. Gandhi was curved upto school books to be read and spoken about at election meetings by power hungry opportunist politicians. This tendency of Gandhi-discard kept going the entire decades of twentieth century. Gandhian austerity and deep concern for the last edge man was no where seen in Nehruvian blueprint of development. Corruption, at every level of system (political, legislative and beaurocratic) has been salient feature of Nehru cult. His extravaganza style of life misguided and provoked the nation towards foul means to fulfill needs of luxury. Basic structure of a healthy nation mainly consists of availability of food, shelter, education, health, and dignity for all, (especially for downtrodden,) has been erased from the Nehruvian development draft. The rift between haves and have - nots has been dangerously widening with every step of poverty eradication which Nehru and following government took. Ironically common man's connectivity with top government agencies grew thinner as people have lost sense of distinction between home or British rule. They survived corrupt system or natural onslaught by themselves. What is justice, legislation and public welfare they don't understand.

As the lower Indian society has been struggling to come to terms with mainstream of nationality, they plunged into US sponsored ghost of globalization and economic liberalization. It offered a dazzle to money hungry Indians to ape to American model of family society and economy. The impact of colonial culture and Eurocentric mindset were yet not eliminated that neocolonialism (Indigenous colonialism) has raised its head in Indian atmosphere. The consequences of which are emergence of new dollar-crorepatis again playing the game of division Briteshers have been playing before transfer of power. Domestic corruption supported and engineered by governmental agencies gravened the problem beyond remedy.

There is a group of people in India having no recorded detail in the books of government activity. They fall under the shadow of negligence, fighting their own way in 'atrocity of nature and constitutional system. British policy then governing India was to divide and rule is enhanced by illegitimate heirs of Britishers by applying lewd tactics. This class of people deprived even of birth and survival right granted by God do not know how harms are planned against them by the very government they contribute by mandating.

Dejection, division and depravation the main features of Indian women society have been the subjects Kamala Das fought to eliminate by pen and person. The story of Indian women as the activist poet Kamala Das saw in post independence was never admittable. For that reason she offered a path way treading on which both male and female can create healthy life style. Condition of Indian women then was like a colony under colony, without anything to claim her own. Her own body was on complete disposal of husband, lover or patriarchal mindset. How will she live, behave and interact was all decided and formulated by colonizing man, 'women are not born they are made in society'. (Symon de Beuvoir–The Second Sex) cast ample light on the degree of plight women undergo by mind and body in due course of their manufacturing.

References and works cited

1. M.K. Naik, *A History of Indian English literature* (Mary Erulkar quoted), p. 208.
2. M.K. Naik, *A History of Indian English literature* (Mary Erulkar quoted), p. 208.
3. *Ibid*, 209.
4. M.K. Naik, *A History of Indian English literature* (Mary Erulkar quoted), p. 210.

5. M.K. Naik, *A History of Indian English literature* (Mary Erulkar quoted), p. 210.
6. R. K. Srinivas Iynagar, *Indian writing in English* (p. Lal quoted), p. 650.
7. N.R. Gopal & Suman Sachar, eds, *Indian English Poetry and Fiction*, (New Delhi: Atlantic Pub. & distrib. 200.0), p. 203.
8. Srinivas Iyengar, *Indian writing in English* (New Delhi: Sterling Pub.) p. 677.
9. *Indian writing in English*, p. 680.

2

Veiled Beauty

Kamala Das as an unbiased reader of contemporary women's mind and body offers not only commentary on the subject but a way out of afflictive surrounding. Each and every line she penned bear true feminist concern. High profile and dogmatic feminist assertions by government office bearers contain no substance except high sounding words. Her sharp critique of hypocritical tendency of male society can be found in every poem. The present poem under analysis 'Sepia' rotates on pivot of one phrase 'Let anger grow like a living sun / and scorch / scorch the very marrow / this sad mouthed human race.' The kingdom of God is dwelt mainly by male and female elements. They are expected to behave on terms of equality coupled with a sense of togetherness but for what unknown reason male understood feminist benevolence, affection and surrender as weakness the natural reason of women's subjections? Kamala Das in utter angry mood declares her refrain from man made social ethics and aesthetics. The poem 'Sepia' is tinged with monolithic tension as the following words reveal:

In noonday queus they dream
of limbs and limousines;
they do no go up the trees

to reach with finger tips
a fringe of summer clouds
they do not go down the sea
count the mermaids eggs
that lie beneath the anemones.

Common habit of males is to possess body, wealth and beauty conventionally available to them but what demands sweating, innovation and exploration they generally avoid. Images of 'limbs and limcusines', 'summer clouds' and 'mermaids eggs' denote points of greed which cannot be achieved as the colonized body of women. Women's body aesthetics has been formulated by man since the immemorial past having no bit of women's paradigm. Kamala Das celebrates women's body as their own territory, spirit and individuality having no sense of male's intervention. Like a knight in battlefield Kamala Das utters the loathsome words.

They are faceless, many cousined,
sad, they rush at every call,
they only sulk in privacy
their religion?
The news - paper hate, the bulge
in Wallets, the scent of morning tea
and of course,
of course, the weekend's
tired lust.

'The weekend's tired lust' motivate man closer to women. Just the lust is quenched they turn face in discard as if she is futile and useless. Mina Surjeet Sing a deep observer of Kamala Das's writing opines what a women and poetry mean to her, "Her poetry seeks to lend voice to the aspirations, desires and plights of the millions of silent women who have not been able to find a voice."[1] In her attempt to give voice to silent women she laid down her life and everything she had.

The poem 'Afterwards' talks of more important role

women often carry without a word of sorrow is motherly burden. Like any other women Kamala Das too had sweet dreams of marriage, husband and children. Hard facts of life shattered her dreams so much so that she started campaigning against convention of Indian marriage. No one can change the course of nature because after marriage child bearing comes. In Indian books of knowledge mother's role in the life of man is highly praised but reality tells the tragic story. In pre - natal condition mother and in-Womb baby talks of love, freedom, music, science and beauty. These things get finished the moment mother has the infant in lap. The cruel reality of life confronts her with all ugliness. In case the infant is a girl the mother's melancholy is on rise. Kamala Das says, "It was normal for a girl to sigh / over a dying bird; / we learnt kindness / as we learnt out books, yes'. Society imposes moral and ethical rules on girl baby more vehementally and hopes to be painstakingly followed. On the other hand that very girl to victimized in the broad day light by masculine attitude and no man comes for help. There is two social and moral scales for men and women judging their deeds and conducts as if women is a creature who does not belong to the men's group. Manju Jaidka's learned study of women's poetry reveals Simone de Beauvior's view of aparthood practice in dealing with women. "one is not born women, one becomes one' says Simon de Beauvoir. The reference here is not to the biological difference but the social discrimination that one must live with".[2]

The images of 'egles fly.' denote hunting tendency of man. The mother Kamala Das and her children were taught to learn the lesson of kindness, delicacy and obedience. The response of male-dominated society was not encouraging, - 'as a little girl I watched / my brothers squate beside a hedge / And slowly blind a beetle'. Even mothers treat male baby more wormly than female because social custom and family tradition are made to run by male babies. Charming description of girl's pain which she had gone through is worth noting.

> The thorny twig in those little hands went quickly red tipped. The insect curled is leg and died I felt sad, but my tears I tried to hide.

Mother is always expected to sacrifice for sons and husband as if sacrifice is alone her moral obligation. The motherly teachings do not grow properly in son. As he grows adult he becomes embodiment of typical man exploiting feminine sentiment. Her poetry always offers a conflict and contrast betweet what is and what should be. Z.M. Molvi, in his article 'Kamala Das : Homeless in the City' examines mood of her poetry thus, "We find a kind of conflict between her ideal desire and the actual or real experience——"[3] Mother finds a lot of satisfaction as the son grows but mother as Kamala Das is, has a fear of getting distanced. Son is heading towards manhood an ancient antagonist gobbling women's feelings. Reproduction of child is a kind of death for mother. As the mother dies the son lives see the agony Kamala Das expresses of son's birth:

> The earth we nearly killed is yours, Now. The flowers bloom again, But savage reds it takes time / to forget blood or the quick of the dying.

She bestows blessings on son who is responsible for her existential death and lose of identity. 'You have to be happy now, / learn to do without love': Son does not appreciates mother's share of contribution in his existence and identity. He wants to be part of exploitative group of males leaving mother alone crying. This attitude of Kamala Das in a message to womenfolk to re-consider their stand and re-make their own anthem of aesthetic. The veiled existence of mother does not help rather create illusion and dilemma. Let the women come to forefront with their new agenda of relationship challenging male run social ethics. Z.F.Molvi studies mother image in the poetry Kamala Das as a fountain of love, "Her search for love is part of a larger quest for motherhood and home which cannot be understood by the commercialized urban sensibility."[4]

Ultimately sons become fathers and mothers dejected lot. Men do not have co-feeling as Kamala Das ironically comments, "there is no song to break your / somnambulistic tread. / You turn like a guilty rot, / And draw your rocky home over you / Like an irremovable shell". So long as mother's lap is a must for new-born's welfare she is valued afterwards sidelined. The extreme selfish attitude of society (husband and son) towards mothers is a point of concern. Kamala Das on her own motherly experience is in a position to suggest women of modern age to create their own path of life shunning centuries old patriarchal norms. Women need to remove veil of ignorance, blind adherence to rotten man - made aesthetic rules for their survival and existence. In the rottening social system Kamala Das finds tears and pains, humiliation and dejection. She writes :

While I was young
From every living moment I wrung only
tears, I was restless,
My thoughts knew no lulls, as tides
That never shrank or grew.
Even fowl had their one - legged sleep. Not
I. How fervently I wished.
That could send those moods flying,

The first person of Kamala Das includes all women treated everywhere in the world on same parameter. Sylvia, Plath, Virginia Woolf, Taslima Nasreen and many more in recent times have raised voice of protest and resentment against anti feminist attitude of contractors of society. How fiery reaction Kamala Das presents by altering Brownian view of God, "God is in his heaven and all / Is right with this stinking world."

"One word 'stinking' used here is enough to open new world's association, from the Gods of Browning to the gods of India."[5] In Kamala Das's observation there are at least two Gods in system : one for male and another for female. Therefore males and females are not trealed on equal scale even in natural matters like food, affection, sexuality and dignity. Kamala Das an ardent advocate fighting the suit of feminism in the court of God and matriarchy argues, "life lay huddled in prisoner's robes / waiting for easy extinction. / I sat in gallery seat and looked / Till my insomniac eyes ached / But that was how I grew."

In the early stage of her confrontation with society she was hoping 'extinction' of feminist prison is possible but as the time went by her hope became fiasco. She concludes that her confinement is endless. "The growth was / Definiteness, the much ironed - folds of a school uniforms", The pre - destined life of Kamala Das has been compared with much ironed school dress which even after getting torn is understandably monotonous, meaningless and unsubstantial. Very soon Kamala Das's dream was shattered, and she came on the ground of hard reality to grapple with, without moaning and undue expectations. Kamala Das's attitude-shift is very much identical to that of Stevie Smith whose poetry, "does not indulge in any kind of whinning or moaning or self pitying angst. It gives evidence of a mind that is always in control of itself and expresses ideas subtly.........."[6]

The concluding part of the poem is a mixture of pathos coupled with future challenge. She is not much expectant of her son because one day he will be and embodiment of his father. Very delicately Kamala Das hints at "your mother groand in labour pain / And slept; and then your first cry rose / To stun the silence of her dreams"; feminist hopes, dreams and desires are to be shattered as Kamala Das's mother had a very dry married life as *My Story* an autobiographical book reveals, 'my mother did not fall in love with my father. They were dissimilar and horribly mismatched."[7] The stories of Kamala Das, her mother and other married women are not different in theme and content, only characters, places, and events change. Kamala Das as a social investigator and feminist crusader has sufficient reasons to conclude that in prevalent scene there is no possibility of compromise between two warring forces.

In the world of masculinity that is also a battlefield there is no time for women to take 'The Siesta' a poem which conveys the theme of struggle women most often get entangled. Her perennial struggle against man-made barriers, according to Kamala Das needs stronger commitment and pointedness. The monotonous life of Kamala Das (as of any women) is a 'sun-lit tank' in which characteristic frailty of 'girl thin limbs played in;' the sun lit tank represents man's world which scotches, bites and stings to girls. No doubt the tank contains 'eels' of delicate nature but they too stare and mock. The description in not only poetically enthralling but realistically telling the cancerous relationship amongst women folk. The feeling of joy or fear as per the condition is suggestive of life and individuality whereas Kamala Das feels 'anonymous peace', an indicator of mortuary peace. Kamala Das wants to nourish her life with energy, enthusiasm, love and better mutual understanding. Her dream of love-life has gone 'pearl-white' that is suggestive of colourlessness. Whom Kamala Das loves as per custom of society is fatal and dangerous. What she feels of her romantic evening is quite reverse in reality. :

> But as evening comes
> snake - like, she sheds
> their silver coils and wakes
> to meet this alien world which talks
> of Gods and casual sin.

Between indefinable 'Gods and casual sins' and removal of 'silver coils' like biting snakes, Kamala Das spoils her life being deprived of love. Her courage to gain identity through 'earthly din' is an utter failure. Her identity is like a 'cut flower' to be removed from vase as it fades. The domestic reality of Kamala Das is identical to almost all women society. They seek love, supporting hand, and sympathizer but what she finds in return is barrenness, deprivation and marginalization in the setup she contributes in the making. She is a gardener, without right to smell even a little bit of fragrance. The following lines reflect the prevalent agony in the life of Kamala Das and fellow women :

fog - eyed, seeking another
to be hers, her own to love
or destroy to share with her
the dim-light gloom where
she moves like a fawn?

The feminist reality Kamala Das paints here appears to be romantic but after close analysis one finds the ugly truth. In introduction to N.V. Raveendsran's book *Aesthetics of Sensuality,* K Ayyappa Panicker generalizes how Kamala Das's protagonists operate within framework of text and outside:

> Kamala Das's protagonist found her relationship with her husband as suitable ground to project her own freedom as being. In the drama of her life with her husband she visualizes herself as a victim of oppression who is tempted to disobey the conventional life he represents. This vision of reality which is related to Kamala Das's aesthetics dominates her poem. Thus in her poems we can see the male characters only in relation to her and not as separate individual.[8]

Kamala Das in her relation with husband is not at ease because conventional mode of relation always tempts to her identity eradication. By raging ideological and realistic war against male exploitation she wants to create a fresh feminist aesthetics freed from centuries old male attitude.

Also, Kamala Das wants to convince whom she can, to admit and honour the aesthetics she intends to create is the content of the poem 'To a Big Brother' (about to be married). In the typical Indian socio-cultural system marriage is a very mysterious institution which makes/mars the life of many. Marriage is a need of individuals as well as society to keep life cycle and social harmony intact but none of these aims are fully met in the real sense. George Bernard Shaw through his protagonists revealed sobbing wedlock's and concluded the truth in this way: 'marriage is a legal prostitution'. The poem is a celebration of 'memory' which Kamala Das keeps alive, her big brother to be married has ignored. The natural difference which distinguishes Kamala Das from her brother is retaining childhood day's sweet reminiscences. Kamala Das has nothing to offer to her big brother on the eve of his marriage except:

> What kind of kids were we?
> I know we sat at windows
> counting cars in Calcutta's Part Street,
> I know we made paper boats and stored them
> in a tin. But do you remember? No?
> Then what can I gift you, I wish I know.

Biologically women have wonderful capability to remember good and bad thingswhich help relationship worm and vibrant. Jane Freedman in her book *Feminism* presents political theorists' opinion underestimating women's capability thus, "political theorists from Plato and Aristotle to Hobbs, Locks and Rousseau argued that a natural difference between men and women, men being naturally more 'rational' and therefore suited to politics and public life, and irrational women being more suited to emotional life of the home."[9] Kamala Das argues here and elsewhere too that women are equal to men in some matters and have larger capacity in handling domestic and emotional affairs where men are absolutely unfit.

The man - women contention in Kamala Das's writing has many aspects. In the purview of man-made aesthetics women are expected to be submissive, charming, and soft spoken, shy benevolent and man-oriented. Any other contrary behaviour on the part of women is considered to be sacriledge and fatal to domestic fabric. The poem under study 'The Fear of the Year' is concerned about seeded fear in the mind of women. Men think of women as 'slow' 'sluggish' 'repetitive' and 'monotonous', they forget about themselves that they are 'selfish', 'exploitative' and 'brute' of these two set of attributes, the feminist one is the least dangerous to the system.

The message of the poem 'The Fear of the Year' is

conveyed by these passages 'Desired on lengths of idle beds / Beside indifferent faces, / For no smile, however fond, can settle time like a paper-wait." The wedlock of Kamala Das has been death lock and her body a 'spicy dish' for her husband. It has momentary use afterwards a worthless object for her husband. The sentiments and feelings of Kamala Das were largely uncared for. The pangs of husbandial humiliation has torn Kamala Das's personality into numerous bits. She as a typical wife is cursed to live in fear. She portrays her state of mind, 'for fear has wraped us all'. Not only Kamala Das but almost all female sentiments are domestically trained to live and die under haunting fear of masculinity. Firstly they are not allowed to dream of freedom, however if freedom comes in distant dream it is dominated by scares of patriarchy. She presents the degree of fear, "In the freedom of our dreams, it / Thrusts its paws to incarnadine / The virgin whiteness so that we / Perceivc the flying steel hands sow / Over mellow cities those dark, / Malevolent seed" :

The description shows miserable domestic and social condition women have to witness in front of 'Steel hand' man. The evil seed of inequality is sown not in a one or two family rather it is a global scene. Sylvia Plath, Stevie Smith and Andriene Rich have expressed almost identical views in their poems :

> She (Stevie Smith) voices her protest against the patriarchal order in a very subtle and civilized manner; there is a genteel quality about Smith's poetry which speaks volumes for culture she was groomed in, the culture she knew she had to conform to in order to survive in a world that was indifferent to women's aspirations.[10]

Kamala Das born in a typical Nair family had due respect for conventions and customs in the earlier days. What she found in return of paying honour was humiliations, physical torture, lose of identity and self-respect. In these painful conditions, she had to re-think and re-frame her stand about relationship with husband and other kith and kins. It is a time to formulate new aesthetics having in mind changed socio-domestic atmosphere of India and abroad, her opinion about husband is subject to incessant change and modification.

In a post-colonial setup she has enlarged her perception from narrow south Indian (Nair) mindset to global citizenship as is evident from 'An Introduction'. She denies her fascination towards corrupt Indian politics, still she knows top Indian politicians from Nehru onwards so routinely as the name of the days. Kamala Das introduces herself in the following way :

> I am Indian,
> born in Malabar, I speak three languages, write in two, dream in one. Don't write in English they cried, English is not your mother-tongue. Why not leave me alone, critics, friends, visiting cousins every one of you?

These words are indicative of Kamala Das's desire for freedom and self - identity. She is herself not bend to lover friend or anybody. Like a Russian poet Akhmatova Kamala Das too raised her voice against inordinate male dominance, "........she raised her voice at a time and in a place where women were not supposed to have a voice, and against powers far too strong for in individual being to fight against."[11]

Male engineered violence and terror against women in family is noway lesser than the state terror. In both cases women are victimized, by loosing identity and voice. Kamala Das' search for voice, identity, aesthetics and selfhood is a kind of endless war against centuries old rottening patriarchal system. The following words show her inherent curiosity to re-create her 'I' defeating negative forces. 'Let me speak / in any I like / The language I speak becomes mine, its distortions, its queerness all mine, mine alone. "Repeated use of mine and I stress the value of Kamala Das's self in the anti-feminist atmosphere. Her use of English for expression of longings is 'honest' and 'human'. Though she has written a large number of short stories in mother-tongue Malayalam where she is a little mechanical than humanly honest in expressing her heart waves. The logic behind use of English Kamala Das advances is understandable:

> You know............
> It voices my longings, my hopes and is useful to me
> as cawing is to crows or roaring to the lions,
> it is human speech, the speech of the mind that is here,........

Speech of mind and heart are basically distinct for Kamala Das. A.N. Durivedi a noted scholar of Indian poetry in English presents Kamala Das's poetic epitome, "Kamala Das is primarily a poet of feminine longings."[12] Longings of a women as Kamala Das is can be expressed only through the language of heart and not otherwise. Whatever feelings of good or bad tastes Kamala Das underwent she wants to utter pertaining her life. "Not the deaf, there / blind speech of trees in storms or of monsoon clouds or of rain / or of incoherent mutterings of the blazing / funeral pyre." The images of 'blind speech of trees', 'monsoon clouds' and 'muttering of blazing funeral pyre' denote sorry state of mind and body which typical Indian women often passes through. As a flag bearing author digging path of life for genral women Kamala Das paints her own adolescent days :

> I grew,
> For I became tall, my limbs swelled and one or two places sprouted hair. When I asked for love, not knowing what else to ask for, he drew a youth of sixteen into his bedroom and shut the door. He did not beat me but my sad.
> Women - body felt too beaten.
> The weight of my breasts and womb crushed me.

Women are women because of her body which crushes it beyond measurement. Popular brand name attached to Kamala Das by all major critics is that she sings and celebrates her 'body' is partially true. In my opinion her celebration of body is for creation of independent feminist aesthetics. The contents of established feminist aesthetics have been formulated by man's selfish and hungry attitude, whereas women were at margin having no say in it. Reacting strongly on man made rule and aesthetics the author asserts, 'Then I wore a shirt / and a black sarong, cut my hair short and ignored all of/ this womanliness.' On the other hand popular male desire is to see women 'Dress (ed) in sari, be girl or be wife, / they cried Be embroider or cook or quarreler / with servants. Fit in, belong, said the categorizers. / Be Amy or be Kamala or better still, be just Madhavikutty. The classic agenda for womenfolk in India is to belong and adjust with categorizers. Any other role which women want to play is sin according to patriarchy. Women cannot express their physical and material needs as it is immoral and an ethical and therefore violence against man made rules. The moral responsibility of women is to satisfy her husband and (sex-partner) by laying down her won needs, whereas her satisfaction in that game has no meaning. This kind of partiality Kamala Das wants to finish by asserting women's equal rights in all matters of life. In India love and marriage are taken identical whereas in reality according to Kamala Das is different. A.N. Dwivedi held :

> In India where love and marriage go hand in hand it is most unfortunate that such a sensitive women as Kamala Das is tied to a stake whence she cannot fly (to use a Shakespearean expression).Such occurrences are not uncommon in the land of Gandhi and Nehru turning many a women tragic and gloomy in their attitude towards life. Kamala Das has made repeated protest against this sort of attitude in her poetry.[13]

She is a warring poet against anti - feminist attitude of society. By this attempt she wants to formulate independent territory of women's aesthetics free from male intervention. She like a pioneer feminist suggests twentieth and twenty first century women, "It is time to choose a name, a role.

/ Don't play a pretending games." In the life of Kamala Das as in any other woman's a man as husband comes to be loved as social a custom. But the same loved one becomes fatal snake for beloved maintains Kamala Das. "Later I met a man. Loved him. Call him / not by an name, he is every man who wants his / women, just as I am every women who seeks love." Male mentality wants women as a dish to enjoy whereas women wants reciprocation of love. She wants to create an atmosphere of mutual love, understanding and co-existence by her total surrender in the hand of husband but she finds dejection, subjection and lose of honour by the same hand. She therefore now does not want agreement or compromise but absolute dischantment from patriarchal web. By two contradictory images she clarifies the position of man and women, "In him the hungry haste of rivers, in me the ocean's tireless, waiting." Mythologically women were compared with 'hungry river' always prone to meet male 'ocean' whereas Kamala Das reversed the situation by glorifying the feminist temperament of patient waiting.

Like existential thinkers she is a ardent advocate of feminist 'I' which is getting tossed and turned in the greedy storm of masculinity. In a very calm mood Kamala Das queries:

> Who are you, I ask each an all.
> The answer is, it is I.
> Anywhere and everywhere I see him who calls himself I. in this world she is tighly packed like sword in its sheath. It is a who drinks a lonely drink new midnight at hotels of strange towns. It is I who make love and then feel shame. It is I who lie dying with a rattle in my throat .... I am a sinner, I am the saint and I am the lover and the beloved..........

The presence of women's 'I' can be witnessed everywhere contributing love, compassion, sex, and everything man needs for survival. Kamala Das stresses the contribution of mother, wife, sister, prostitute, dancer, beggar, and beloved in making man what he is now. Despite all sacrifices women make are called 'sinner' according to Hindu, Christian, Islam and other schools of religion, of which Kamala Das is critical. In the end of each women comes hopelessness and marginalization. "We share the same name (to use Shakespearean phrase frailty thy name is women) the same fate, the same crumbled dreams."

"Suffering and unhappy ending are still considered as its essential indegrients according to Indian and western theoreticians of aesthetics."[14] Says A.N. Dwivedi about Kamala Das's contents of poetry. Having offered her and women folk's introduction Kamala Das now describes blood relationship and its multiple characteristics. The most reliable relationship in human life is blood-relationship but as far as women's welfare is concerned by sons and grandsons it is very doubtful in the modern socio - domestic contexts.

The poem 'Blood' is a little nostalgic and autobiographical. Kamala Das has great attachment towards her grandmother's way of interaction. The mother sentiment is always loving, caring and compassionate about family children and household commodities. In every thing they have bought or built visualize their own image. Destruction of that thing is personal lose for mother says Kamala Das in the following lines :

> You see this house of ours
> Now three hundred year old,
> it's falling to little bits
> before our very eyes.
> The walls are cracked and torn
> And moistened by the rains,
> The tiles have fallen here and there
> The windows whine and graon.

The above lamentation of grandmother to granddaughter (Kamala Das) is suggestive of women's preserving and maintaining temperament which by and large men lack. The crumbling house can be interpreted as symbol of women's body and existence which always confronts man's negligence and insult. Rats, snakes and other insects have taken shelter in the house once loved and adequately maintained by Kamala Das's grandmother. The following lines have metaphoric significance hinting at man - women's poisonous relationship, "And all the snake-Gods in the shrine/ Have lichen on their hoods." The "hooded snake" stands for male which creeps the area women have maintained by hard labour. The house now crumbling, captured by snake - Gods was dearly loved by grandmother. Kamala Das plans to re - built grandmother's house because she says, "I love this house."

As kamala Das's grandmother was fed on God so it seems almost all women are God fearing that makes them coward and escapanist. No exploitative move that man has started women can thwart away because of rotten religious upbringing. This stalemate Kamala wants to erase from contemporary women's mind. Selfish religion and misinterpretation of God have worsened the feminist position in Indian society and family. "All her feasts were monotonous / For the only dish was always God. / And rest mere condiment."

Childhood days memory of grandmother and that of Kamala Das are in some ways identical as both loved elephant-ride and had fascination for jewel-box. Kamala Das used to listen enchanting stories of grandmother narrating the princely marriage who died soon after marriage leaving the princes desperately alone is an echo of any women's personal life. Grandmother was proud of her family-blood as the oldest and grandest in the locality. As the time went by things changed and family honour started getting reduced.

Women community is taught by patriarchal system to be of compromising temperament. Despite having made various compromises she became nothing but a heap of frustration and bundle of futility. Women suffer physically and mentally having not even lover or husband to sympathize at the time of anguish. Kamala Das as a voice of women society admits, "I had learnt by then / Most lessons of defeat." Defeat and regression is the lesson women are bound to accept. There is a lot of affinity between Kamala Das's concept of women subjection and that of Margaret Atwood. She in her essay "Survival" explains, "what is the victim's response to oppression? It is a passive acceptance or is there some kind of resentment."[15] At a stage of emotional exuberance Kamala Das feels the grandmother's house to be grandmother herself. It is not romanticization of hard feminist reality but overflow of inner feelings :

For I thought I saw the windows close
Like the closing of the eyes
I thought I heard the pillars groan
And the dark room heaves a sigh.

Kamala Das under the necessity left grandmother's house at the disposal of 'snake-Gods : Flower and herbs grandmother reared were left alone along with the confronting. Arabian sea's fascination. Construction and destruction is the law of nature therefore she patiently admits decaying house. What hurts Kamala Das is grandmother's undervaluation by family members. She paints the ruin - scene thus :

From every town I iive in
I hear the rattle of its death
The noise of rafters creaking
And the windows whine.
I have let you down
Old house I seek forgiveness
O mother's mother's mother.
I have plucked your soul.

Death of grandmother and decay of ancestral house is symbolic of fall of feminist identity and eradication of existence. The last lines of the poem take readers back to the memory lanes where grandmother used to go for elephant ride and Shiva-worship. The poem concludes with a tone of apology from Kamala Das's part as she is unable to protect her grandmother's house which sheltered "The oldest blood in the world."

Kamala Das is proud of her geographical topography and of that too which bounty nature has gifted. The poem "A Hot Noon in Malabar" offers scenic and social truth of Malabar people which empowered Kamala Das's imagination to go deep in the psyche of protagonists. The climatic harshness most visibly impacts the life of surface people. "This is a noon for beggars with whining / voices, a noon for men who come from hills ...." Kamala Das's view stretches from road realities to psychic evils rampant in the mind of men. A big bunch of poor people gather along the roads to make both ends meet by selling bangles, reading for tune - cards, facing humid weather of Malabar almost bare-bodied and empty belly. Such people are "all stained with time, for brown kurava girls / with old eyes." The contrast of "old eyes" with young "Kurava girls" is an effective comment on social reality Kamala Das has deep and factual understanding of social - political truths of Indian soil. Her autobiographical story - cum - essay "A poet at the hustings" narrates real story of a women's pangs :

> ....no political party ever thought of the under - privileged except as material for their new slogans. Eradicate poverty screamed the media I wanted to tell the politicians just listen to the poors, lend them your ears. The women embraced me with emaciated arms and wept on my shoulder. Forgetting shame I wept with them.[16]

Real story which Kamala Das narrated is no way different from what he poetically portrays. "Noon" has different meanings for different people. It is painful experience for under privileged lying roadside and for privileged it is a chance to exploit poor lot by offering fake sympathy. See the difference two edges of Indian (Malabar) society come across with :

> This
> Is a noon for strangers with mistrust in their
> eyes, dark, silent, ones who rarely speak,

At all, so that when they speak,
Their voices run wild, like jungle - voices
Yes, this is
A noon for wild men, wild thoughts
Wild love.

Above lines denote cryptic message of "noon" for two distinct classes of society. A. N. Dwivedi underlines the basic features of Kamala Das's poetry in the following observation which above description also justifies, "Kamala Das's poetry abounds in details of misery and grief, loneliness and helplessness, death and disease coldness and frigidity, frustration and dejection and all there render her vision tragic."[17]

The society which is thoroughly fragmented cannot hope cohesion and aesthetic integrity at surface for this reason Kamala Das wants to re-construct her feminist society on its won doctrine and day to day practices absolutely distinct from male-intervention. The poem that follows is a pathetic fable of a domestic maid servant popularly addressed as "Nani" who survives on the thrown out pieces of bread of that family which she supports by body and mind. The luck of such women is well understood in the post modern Indian society where women (Nanis) are easily digestible property for job providing male - dominating families. The consequences of such women Kamala Das knows well, "the pregnant maid hanged herself in the privy one. For three long hours / until the police came." The dead sentiment of family members towards Nani (now-dead) and intervention of police is sufficient indicator of future course of action. By way of her own reaction the poet offers generally passive attitude towards such tragic events:

She was hanging there
a clumsy puppet, and when the wind blew
Turning her gently on the rope, it seemed
To us who were children then that Nani
Was doing, to delight us, a comic dance.

The common view about maid servants is India and abroad is very despicable which Kamala Das censors. Her own opinion is not only healthy but worth prevailing in the society she plans to formulate, after unknown death of Nani in a privy was largely abandoned by all family member. In the writing of Kamala Das memory of lovable things play very crucial role as the following lines dismantle:

> Another
> Year or two and I asked my grandmother one day
> don't you remember Nani
> ....
> Grandmother
> Shifted the reading glasses on her nose and stared
> at me Nani? asked who is she?
> With that question ended Nani.

Neglecting even the memory of an active women (Nani) by grandmother is fatal indicator of receding women's welfare in society. What we routinely encounter in family and society is an instance of women slaughtering women. Very effectively kamala Das attracts the attention of readers towards feminist fact in contemporary society:

> It is this designed
> deafness that turns mortality into
> immortality, the definite into
> the soft indefinite.

Attentiveness and showing genuine worry by women folk for themselves is the demand of the changing global nature. Self negligence proves to be more fatal than masculine strategy against women. The world is broadly divided into battlefield one side women fighting for their cause in front of fortified masculine territory. Putting the position of women in the terms of W.B. Yeats matter becomes more transparent, "Poets, held Yeats; are like 'women who labour to be beautiful" and here is a women poet who has known through the years how to labour and how to be beautiful."[18] This opinion of A.N. Dwivedi justifies the argument I raised in the analysis of the poem "Nani" that women laying down their lives and in return finding nothing but blasphemy and allegation. The binding lines of he poem show the thematic and stylistic grace of the poem. :

> They are lucky
> who ask questions and move on before
> the answers come, those wise ones who reside
> in a blue silent zone, unscratched by doubts........
> ---------------------------
> in life like music in the koel's eggs like lust in the blood or like sap in tree.

Kamala Das argues that all their life women sacrifice their body, soul and self respect for the welfare of family but in the end they get humiliation and pangs of marginalization. In entire social structure women's contribution is larger than that of male's however they are the least recognized and focused in different aspects of life. Mother-image is very significant in the formation of 'males' who claim their leading role only on the ground of physical strength as means of oppression and exploitation. The structures of society (individuals, families organizations etc) find working energy not by corporal strength but by emotion, feelings, love, understanding, and cooperation the basic attributes of females. The following poem "My Grandmother's House" discusses the issue of women's (Grandmother's) contribution in making house abounding in love, faith, care, co-operation which are also the salient features of Kamala Das's view of contemporary aesthetics. The concept of body beauty has been integral part of imperial and feudal psyche. Now in an age of democratic system feudal parameter of aesthetics does not prevail. The hollow, wrinkled and gnarled body of Grandmother has all aesthetic values which Kamala Das focuses at. The present poem seems sequel of "Blood" in which memory of caring grandmother haunts Kamala Das.

She has no option or substitute of grandmother, whereas through other ways she is socially esteemed, financially sound, yet grandmother's absence pains her. "The women (grandmother) died / the house withdrew into silence, snakes moved among the books. I was then to young to read." The stylistic and thematic excellence of Kamala Das must be underlined over here in the use of "snake" moving into "books" she could not study then. The "snakes" stand for men and "books" for knowledge being hegemonized by males forbidding women's access. The feminist position in third world countries is miserable. See the poetic transversion of the same. :

> How often I think of going there,
> to peer through blind eyes of windows or
> just listen to the frozen air
> or in the wild despair, pick an armful of
> darkness to bring it here to lie
> behind my bedroom door like brooding
> dog …… .

The women community inhibited of "book" (knowledge), "house" (love) has nothing to imbibe but "wild despair" and lastly "an armful of despair". The desperation women are bound to undergo is not natural but man-manufactured maintains Kamala Das. In the system of nature both male and female deserve equal status and treatment but Linda Hutcheon puts the matter in her book *"The Politics of Post Modernism* in the favour of feminist cause. "Produced discourses which often sustain male privilege - feminize desire - its satisfaction, its objects may need re-thinking-especially to consider what Catherine Stimpson calls its heterogeneity."[19]

Women's distinction is understood by the world only for sexist purposes. As far as their 'esteem' and 'heterogeneity' are concerned nobody seems bothering. Kamala Das in the text of the poem focuses the point. "I who have lost / my way and beg now at stranges doors / to receive love, at least in small change."

Once the women is de - centralized for her individual requirements (shelter, food, love honour) she can go to any extreme to fulfil her 'needs' having no heed to what hypocrite male mind utters. Munshi Premchandra's immortal character "Budhi Kaki" (the aged aunt) is real state portrayal of hypocrisy man - woman rottening relationship show. How can one hope of compassionate response from women (it may be Kamala Das, Budhi Kaki or any household voiceless woman) against selfish and immoral treatment men offer to women. The poem "Pigeons" presents a mystic and metaphoric atmosphere. In Indian line of discourse "Pigeons" symbolize peace and stability which is absent in the life of women. It is a distant dream women cannot afford to access, Kamala Das describes, "Pigeons on the ledge / of an afternoon dream / sit strangely silent". The silent sitting of pigeon is a dream of afternoon not reachable. Ironically "hot dust rises / falls on sun-pealed beaks / on the city of fevered lanes." Whatever be the facts of women's life 'dream' for better days is always on function. Kamala Das despite numerous desperation hopes for better dreams to come to reality:

> The sun swell. Then
> Swollen like a fruit
> it runs harsh silver threads
> lengthwise my afternoon
> dream.

Dreams and hopes are that essence of Kamala Das's life which empowers, encourages and motivates to keep fight on in all affliction, Gayatri Spivak Chakravarty wirtes that, "Between patriarchy and imperialism, subject constitution and object formation the figure of women disappears.............."[20] The disappearing figure of women is a great threat for allocation of identity, existence and formation of aesthetic outline.

The poet's worry for women's narrow place in patriarchy is evident from every poem she has penned so far. "The wild Bovgainvillae" is a symbolic representation of women (here

Kamala Das) in an alien surrounding. Men find adjustment sooner than expected but women are ever on margin because of 'body' and innate compassion. They are ever on danger zone because of victimizing masculine look and attitude. The poem is in Calcutta once familiar but currently strange. The mental unease persists in night as the poet reveals :

> Days
> When even my bed gave
> No rest, but like a troubled sea tossed me on
> Its waves, and how I groaned
> And moaned, and constantly yearned for a man from
> Another town ....

Desire of a 'protecting man' by a women is ancient fact but in the changed context 'protector' has become 'hunter' - the fact Kamala Das known better than any body else. Initially she seems of compromising, adjusting and synthesizing temperament but finding no one fits for the job she turns her focus to conflict and self-identification. Her journey of self-discovery is charged with negation of masculinity and rotten socio - religion - political systems. She wants to lay foundation of new feminist ideology which is self - inspired having no respect for monolithic methods. In her excursion she finds :

> It is a good world, and
> Packed with distraction. I walked through streets beside
> The sea, where the barges
> Float, their undersides rotting and the garbage
> Rot and the dead fish rot,
> And I smelt the smell of dying things and the
> Heavy smell of rotting
> Dead.

The two pictures- one of 'Sea' having floating boad and the second of 'underside' of barges, 'garbage', 'dead fish', 'dying things' denote the stagnation of physique and mind. The beautiful is flowing, changing and renovating and ugly is stagnant, rigid, repulsive and moving back. These two conditions constitute, according to Kamala Das, what is aesthetically appreciable and what not. P.B. Shelley in his *"Ode to the West Wind"* heralds before the rotting world that "If winter comes can spring be far behind", the answer is not, the spring is nearby. Dead and rotten things need quick removal from the stem of society and individual advocates Kamala Das. In the present poem the image of 'sea' serves the purpose of 'freshness and renewal' which Devender Kohli also notices, "The image (sea) serves scorching world of the sun. Sea imagery is part of Kamala Das's elemental symbolism."[21]

Next obtrusive imagery Kamala Das offers has double meaning. Firstly it contrast with Kamala Das's desired life of women symbolically told by "Bougainvillea" and secondly the severe problem of prostitution in major metropolis of world (here Calcutta). :

> I walked the street where the night girls with sham
> Obstrusive breasts sauntered
> And yellow lamps, up and down wandered
> Beaming their sickly smiles
> At men. And on streets near old cemeteries
> Where the dead are so dead
> That even their tombstones have lost their name in
> That rains, and are pale now ....

An open demarcation between alive and dead, beautiful and ugly and admittable and rejectable is a must according to author otherwise an atmosphere of illusion and dissonance will seize the entire society. The grotesque and obtrusive elements tend to fuse with nice that obstructs the observation of the poet as what is beautiful and what otherwise? The decayed and yellowed tombs have lost grace but beside that blooms "Marigold and wild Bougainvillea" the indicators of emerging fresh contemporary life. :

But, I did see beside
The older tombs some marigolds
And the wild red bougainvillea
Climbing their minarets. I walked, I saw,
I heard the city tamed
Itself for me, and then my hunger for a
Particular touch waned...... .

The city of Calcutta which was callous and untamed for the author changed its attitude where she investigated the smooth and coarse corners of life consequently finding spring of marigold and bougainvillea for herself. Adverse and regressive condition of human life change to positivism once you began confronting things indiscriminately. Like P.B. Shelley, Walt Whitman and Thom Gunn, Kamala Das tries to cope with the multiplicity of world in its totality. As a synthesis, A.N. dwivedi concludes "Kamala Das is primarily a poet of feminist longings. ....she appears as a champion of women's cause"[22]

The poem "Forest Fire" externalizes the poet's fume on rotten customs of society and civilization of which she is a victim. The words 'of late I have begun to feel hunger .... like a forest-fire' forcefully indicates the revengeful mind of the author. The heterogeneous and anti - women surroundings which have grown on over the centuries, Kamala Das wants to burn to ashes as forest-fire does. She wants to become a killer of discordant social traits which let not feminism develop at natural pace. She imagines growth of women's welfare same as "Bald child in / open pram: suddenly the poet diverts her attention from innocent child in cart to :

Slim lovers behind the tree and you, old
Man with paper in you hand and sunlight in
Your hair ....

These lines are open comments on factual details Kamala Das has been coming across with in different cities. What attracts in this poem is, :

My eyes lick at you like flames, my nerves
consume; and when I finish with you in the
Pram, near the tree, on the park bench I spit
Out small heaps of ash, nothing else.

The fiery attitude of kamala Das wants to burn down all barriers in the way of her dream-world. Her reaction is not only decaying but she wants to re - construct society on the scale of equality for women in all affairs of life. I find in writings of Kamala Das Shelley like iconoclastic attitude. But what she confesses as a social activist is hopeful, "But in me / The sights and smells and sounds shall thrive and go on / and on an on." Like metaphysical poets Kamala Das also wants to focus on nature gifted instincts such as sight (eye), smell (nose), sound (ear) as elements of existence and individuality equating herself with men. Moreover she keeps her innocence intact despite un warranted intrusion of negative forces. She admits "In me shall sleep the baby / That sat in prams and sleep and wake and smile its' / Toothless smile". The society and nature maintains Kamala Das is at war against feminist welfare. Arlence R.K. Zide holds that "Kamala Das's theme transcends the 'personal' because what she attempts to poeticize is universal experience of women".[23] Women as cozy beautifier of husband's intimate moments is expected to be honey-tongued, lavish and everyway lovable, which all women try to groom themselves as per husbandial expectations. Having consumed the 'dish of woman's body' they discard and condemn it. The lines Kamala Das writes are tragic in mood but aggressive in action. :

In me shall walk the lovers, hand
In hand, and in me, where else the old shall sit
And feel the touch of sun. In me, the street - lamps
Shall glimmer, the cabaret - girls cavort, the
Wedding drums resound, the eunuch swirl coloured
Skirt and sing sad songs of love.........

The women are expected to contain multi - faceted roles in their single body unit. Classic Indian text "Kamsutra" of Acharya Vatsyayan assigns obligations on typical Indian women to be mother in kitchen, whore on bed, friend in social affairs, whereas the same text is mute about man's duties towards better half. A pedantic thinker Rousseau who advocated freedom for all as nature has granted is against liberty of women. " ....it seemed perfectly evident that 'nature herself has decreed that women, both for herself and for her children should be at the mercy of man's judgement."[24] Pruning the wings of feminist flight is not acceptable to Kamala Das as she has examined every corner of existent relationship for reciprocal understanding. She has met with "the wounded moan,/ and in me the dying mother with hopeful / Eyes shall gaze around ...." Kamala Das having worn the costume and genuine character of baby girl and her innocence, robust wife's sexual exuberance, friend's mutuality and honest citizen's dutifulness towards male mindset is certainly an object of cheating and betrayal. Thus, she has left any hope of honest relationship from the male partners. Any move to forge an understandable connection with male agents is a fiasco; the idea is poetically rendered in "The Relationship". The relation vitally exists when both partners stand fidel and true of words and deeds for each other. The concluding line of the poem candidly indicates what really happens in the society, "That I shall find my rest, my sleep, my peace / And even death nowhere else but here in / my betrayers arms........." How paradoxical life women are destined to spend in society. Whom they love by body and soul ardently, they cheat. The condition of suffocation and voicelessness Kamala Das wants to dismantle by adding strong and meaningful voice to their "body" and "soul". Like Robert Browing Kamala Das celebrates her body value than mere ideation like romantics. Man's antipathy and reluctance towards benevolent women is a miserable experience Kamala Das does not want to tolerate any longer. "Anti-ethical attitude of man and women play an important role in the construction of Kamala Das's imagery. That her poetic imagination, to a considerable extent is based on sexuality.[25] The history of male - female intimacy is as old as nature itself and since then women have been yearning for a genuine partner. She in return finds, "saddened centuries". The author further says :

> Yes
> It was my desire that made him male
> And beautiful, so that when at last we met
> To believe that once I knew not his
> Form, his quite touch, or the blind kindness
> Of his lips was hard indeed.

Kamala Das's own life events do show the "blind kindness of his (husband's) lips" that was not erotic rather hard and despicable. Being a postmodern poet Kamala Das created "new space for herself and contemporaries on women's body relation with men, the issue has been mostly forbidden in generation that went by. Social and physical relation between man and women is not achievement in itself rather a means to find meaning for life. Jai Krishna Nair held that ".........for Kamala Das love is not an end in itself, the culmination of it is the achievement of a meaning for life that is not to be found in the present modes of modalities."[26]

Kamala das wants to re define man-woman relationship on the pedestal of equality, empathy and co-existence. Any other kind of relation which subjugates and humiliates woman is fake and fraudulent. The following unpublished poem "The High Tide" is a verbal manifestation of lover's excitement over unknown knocking at the gate. Different moods and whims Kamala Das has been facing of her husband since the date of marriage.

She ironically calls her husband, "The king had lost his power." The implied meaning reveals that masculine dominance is shrinking giving place to new strength of feminism. Like an exhausted Satan he shouts at wind knocking at the gate. The author presents an imbalanced mental state of husband. For no apparent reason "the sea (metaphor for husbands fuming mind) is wild / This morning, there is perhaps a high tide on." In the meantime telephone rings causing additional irritation which comes out in the shape of abusive language. Notable is the use of ugly world of defeated king and gradually winning beloved's stance.

> What idiot, he says
> Grief-lichened, his voice is thicker, it run so harsh that even
> The poetess now turns her face away who loves him
> Without rhyme or reason— — — — —

In a round about fashion the poet poses very paining question before the lost king, "What has happened / to the dancing girls; what has happened to the cringing crowd?" The question leads readers to understand the hollowness of king's character. Having a wife at home does not quench his carnal desire that's why "dancing girls" are desires. Such a dirty and flippant character cannot find inner peace in wife's company is sure to poke mouth here and there unscrupulously. The conclusion reached at on the ground of this poem shows that male characters generally deviate from moral path of life, on the other hand expects high fidelity from womenfolk. The conflict of moral characters (of man and women) Kamala Das focuses lucidly, "we find a kind of conflict between her ideal desire and the actual or the real experience both in her married life."[27]

Fastly altering moods and position in married life of author lead her to peep through "The Corridors" of mind for solace and satisfaction. In the entire gamut of writing Kamala Das always looks hungry for a house which has peace, love, and stability of mind coupled with body. She most often asks herself. :

> Why do I so often dream
> Of a house where each silent
> Corridor leads me to warm
> Yellow rooms - and, loud voices

Welcome me, and rich friendly
Laughter's...... .

Kamala Das, like any other woman wants to be part and parcel of that family unit which lovingly pours, "Friendly laughter's in "warm yellow rooms". The desire of Kamala Das is not unnecessary and unquenchable but reality of her life is contrary. There is an unbridgeable gap between feminist expectation and hard familial truth. So, she laments:

.........but I do
Not seem to recollect name
Or the real nature of their
Relationship with me?

In the crowd of society genuine relationships have lost their value and validity. Creating social relation is easier than keeping them alive, hence it is imperative of every individual to be true and faithful to relation ship, maintains Kamala Das, Z.F. Molvi comments what house and relation mean to Kamala Das. "Her search for love (husband - wife, mother - son etc.) is a part of larger quest for motherhood, and 'home' which cannot be understood by the commercialized urban sensibility. The urban experience in Kamala Das constitutes his sense of conflict and anguish."[28]

Even after spending a long life of devotion women are strangers in the family she nurtures of her blood and feelings. The tone of Kamala Das is very pathetic and gloomy in these words, "why do I remain ever a stranger" in the mob of relations. They all recognize for greed only, having their requirements fulfilled they turn their faces aside in disgust.

The humiliation of women goes on for ever to the extent that she becomes devoid of self-identity and esteem. She narrates, "Once awake, I / see the bed from which my love / Has fled, the empty room the / Naked walls............." The flying of love from her bed, "the empty room" and naked walls" are reflective of lose of author's identity and existence in a world of her own. Like J.P. Sartre, the author also worries about existential dilemma which captures all women in contemporary social setup. Sharda Iyer's study of Kamala Das from this paradigm is commendable, "She makes a discovery of human existence and narrates her experiences vividly and passionately. She rejects masks and roles and refuses to accept the limitation of her biology."[29]

Traditionally women's biology and monolithic patriarchal attitude do not allow any women to talk of "empty bed" on the pretext of pseudo morality. Men have granted undue liberty of doing and saying for themselves which Kamala Das equates by making bold and frank statements uncaring what social fabric responds to unusual manner of her frankness certify her role as a maker of contemporary women's aesthetics. Under the veil existence which women had been tolerating so far needs, a quick and bold thwart so that their inherent energy of body and soul could be put in use asserts the author. But the authoritative wall of restrictions is everywhere. Women do not know what they are for? The repenting and protesting voice of Kamala Das utter. :

> Like an imposter, watching
> The crowd who welcome me - and
> Know, deep inside the truth that
> They know me by another
> Name - a well - loved name I am
> Powerless to recollect ?

In the war of feminist cause Kamala Das finds herself sometimes feeble and some times full of stamina as the opposite party is historically tactful in crookedness. However, the struggle Kamala Das has launched as a mission is to go on until destination is arrived at, and that is removal of black-veil from the mind and body of women. The author's movement is not an easy one but a challenge to the authority of contractors of society. The tone of challenge is perpetuated in the following poem "I Shall Some Day" in which Kamala Das says that she has studied her life in the world and that of other women and has concluded to remove the 'Cocoon' (veil) from their face. Men have covered the face of women for enhancement of beauty and also keeping them ignorant. Veils and flirting-words flung on women are illusion and misguiding the poet asserts:

> I shall some day take
> Wings, fly around, as often petals
> Do when free in air, and you dear one,
> Just the sad remnant of a root, must
> Lie behind, sans pride, on double bed
> And grieve,

The poet's desire to fly like bird and petals in sky is suggestive of realizing one's own potential in addition to investigating pros and cones of the region. This enthusiastic move of the poet may or may not be rewarding however journey enriches the totality of experience. After all she wants to achieve freedom, self - respect and individuality that all have been diminished to a dangerous level. Since Kamala Das is an anti - romantic author believing not only in sky and flight, assures her kith and kin, "I shall some day return." In the flight she can face "hurt by wind, sun and rain, / Too hurt by fierce happiness ...." But utopian fly does not pay adequately therefore she promises return to earth (reality) where she has to fight by body and soul. "I shall some day see / My world, de - fleshed, de-veined, de-blooded / Just a skeletal thing." She knows the truth of shelter but in the "nest of familiar scorn ...." The poem is an indictor of Kamala Das's shift from patriarchal custom to new mode of life style which women like Kamala Das have pledged to beat out. Anne Sexton's and Kamala Das's "work shows an awareness of the methods by which women are brainwashed by patriarchy, the way they internalize the male morns and attitudes, deliberately ignoring their won gender and it's special needs."[30] The poem concludes with a typical Indian tone of husbandial "scorn" for wife. This scornful atmosphere is the ultimate shelter of wife in traditional Indian family.

Scorn, hatred and humiliation have been different coloures of tragic life of women. Kamala Das offers a pen - picture of a "Drama" which the body and life of women have been participating from pretty long time. Like a skilled dramatist she presents stage spectacles.

> ....drafty stage
> With bleary flood light, wooden boards,
> And just a red - red lamp above
> Like an angry sun and a huge
> Untagged bouquet lying behind.........

In the above mentioned artificial, monotonous and breathe suspending atmosphere Kamala Das (bride) enters in the family of husbands. The day she stepped in her confidence began slowly dying. She is the main character of tragedy and the play is about to begun on her body, mind, soul, and existence. She is blackened, from inside out as he confesses, "Black gowned, black veiled / And wail and beat my breast." Having faced the black reality of present life she burst out like a volcano, " I am wronged, I an wronged I am so wronged ...." The atmosphere and temperament of husbands family is gloomy and anti-bride. All members to Kamala Das appear as butchers. :

> Then at me from rows and rows of
> Cavernous mouths where reason died
> A hundred deaths, the laughter rose
> Like locust hunger .... they said, ha
> ha ha ha ....

Very soon the author felt the futility of matrimonial festivity. She is tired of 'nothingness' that is inherent in the ceremonious nature of marriage. She notes that fact from her parental marriage, "My mother did not fall in love with my father, they were dissimilar and horribly mismatched."[31] Dissimilar and mismatched marriages do not succeed. In most of the cases husband alone plays the "Cavernous" role as the author concludes :

When I speak
My lines, though his lips do no move
I hear him laugh ha ha ah ha
ha ha ....

Insult by husband Kamala Das tolerated many a time that it became permanent feature of her life. She passed at several occasions through physical and psychic ailments which for husband and other male members of family was unserious matter. The practice of incessant negligence by relatives turned Kamala Das more and more self-reliant and self-contained energy capable of breaking the fence of orthodox and conservative mindset. In the poem "After the Illness" she recalls familial and husbandial reluctance that every woman invariably comes across with. "Illness" as the poem suggests is not an outside phenomenon falling on the body of women but the body and general life of women itself is illness which she cannot shed off. Illness entails death in general presumption but women's life complexity as the author notes "There was then no death, no end", that means that women have to live in diseased condition for ever. "The weary body settling into accustomed grooves / And, he said, his soft suffering face against my knee / I willed it so." For women "death" is preferable than diseased domestic life as it unleases freedom from relational suffocations. Women's uneasiness serves as a subject of men's enjoyment. The lover / husband "noticed the high greens of my illness". The greens in illness is a contrasting situation women often witness in their matrimonial or general life. The poetic rendering of mental and corporal facts of average women's life is stunning.:

..........the bones
Turning sharp beneath the dry loose skin, the yellowed eyes
The fetid breath and the prayers to unfamiliar Gods.

The above facts show how negligence and uncare have reduced women to existential nothingness and corporal hollowness. Kamala Das ironically puts question before her husband, "Did he feel neglect while? battled with my pain"? Because of prolong illness her body became "unfit" to satiate husband's flesh hunger. The energy of body is fled off leaving Kamala Das a shadow. Her conjugal relation was a fiasco as in "*My story*" she confesses, "*My story*" tells us repeatedly that her marriage floundered on the rocks of mind right form the start,"[32] and again "...........her marriage was doomed to fail from the beginning ....her husband was immersed in his office-work ....dinner ....followed by sex.........."[33] Her personality, moods and sentiments were largely sidelined by the husband and family whom she devoted with all she had.:

> Without health's
> Anointments was numb and unhearing what lusted then
> For him, was it perhaps the deeply hidden soul?

For husband's hunger wife's robust body means all, "not deeply hidden soul." Kamala Das wants to castigate the vulture's attitude of men towards women. The prose-poem that follows now is "Sunset, Blue Bird" is an open-heart commentary on her lover's horrible presence in the company of other chaps. In between the friendly conversation Kamala Das grew pale and sick by recalling the memory of husband. He is a horrible ghost always haunting the mind and body of author. Her moods and mind go changed by the name of husband only. A.N. Dwivedi rightly recalls, "Kamala Das is a poet of moods and freaks......"[34] she is extremely afraid of "king" the husband "I was warned not to near the king but I did go and believe me he was like a man like any man, he clutched me to his breast, he said he loved me I was happy and thought he was happy too.........."

After some year of conjugal intimacy Kamala Das had beautiful baby of her husband and after that rift developed between the two. Now her physical charm does not enthrall him, "he no longer calls for me, he no longer comes to me............" What evil has infected the body and soul of Kamala Das that she is suffering the pangs of husbandial negligence? Not because of infatuation but vaulting hatred Kamala Das, "sees him every where ......sees him in every thing like a blue bird at sunset he flits across my sky". In third world countries like India women are regulated and controlled in every affairs of life by illogical customs the issue centuries back Rousseau too argued, "women were the 'precious half of the republic', they made the customs (rather customs made them) while men made the laws. Thus women should limit themselves to domestic governments."[35] (husband related affairs)

This proposition of Rousseau that man and women have respective fields to work within and the violation of that boundary is naturally undesirable is strongly opposed by Kamala Das. Along with feminist issues which have been in debate for pretty long time, the author records natural and topographical detail which she dwelt around Malabar. The weather of Malabar is wet and marshy described in "The Swamp". It presents locality and Kamala Das's emotional response to it which she roamed about wildly since the early days of life.

The cracks on the earth have caused pain in the foot - sole of the author. The physical pain passes on in the form of lover's reluctance. "......he undressing my soul effortlessly blindly reaching the locus of anguish ...." Life of a woman in typical Hindu society is an epic of "locus of anguish" be it Sita, Draupadi, Ahalya or recent women Kamala Das etc. Their grieves have root in the cancerous social setup which goes up itself stirred by circumstances. It is customary in our society to introduce a marriageable girl in the following prose-poetic phraseology of Kamala Das, ".........Virtue is the richest jewel said my grandmother she wore such invisible jewel..............." The honest Kamala Das has objection to what her grandma said in eulogy of her corporal grace, "I was born fair but within weeks like the rolled gold bangles on the servant's arms my skin grew tarnished. I was the first dark girl in the family ...." The poet's confession of personal reality and refusal of grandma's hyperbolic praise certify her transparent nature.

The author's tragedy not only pertains to physique but to mind and soul. Several times she had been in hospital's boring atmosphere for months along. Kamala Das had to go multiple pangs, one of son's separation, husband's negligence and bodily pain. Nancy Chorodov refutes mother-image as natural and blessing in her book *The Reproduction of mothering* (1978). "She rejects the idea that mothering is an innate, natural instinct................"[36]

After choosing to be mother women have to rotate blindly on narrow domesticity unconditionally. Kamala Das's pinpointing to lover's selfish attitude makes Jane Freedman's viewpoint justified, The poet says, "my beloved is armed with cunning and violent hates and mistrusts ....I call him my baby I hold him to my breast............ I am silent and in silence move away." Even in unsound health Kamala Das paid proper attention to husband's carnal needs, still his stand is static and mechanical towards surrendering wife. In the mind of mother stays the variety of roles which women carry in their life time. "Charadov argues that the desire to mother is part of the desire to be feminine which girls pick up at early age."[37] This psychopathic ordeals which all women pass through are symbolically depicted in the realistic details of Malabar swamps:

> I am the tainted bush the poisonous snakes retreat at three am.............. I have no name of my own and my past is a desolate terrain where memory like tall trees grown ...... on hot rooms the devil dancers came

"The swamp" outside is located also in the mind of author with all characteristics. Like a cinema screen pictures run through the mind of Kamala Das. To exhibit her distaste she pours poisonous words for husband :

> He is the richest the strongest the
> Deadliest I lit one thousand and one

> Lamps at out snake shrine praying for a mate ....(Kamala Das's anger grows high) I shall rise one day I shall stalk out of his bed one day I shall sleepwalk along the marine drive he will be then just another man just another season...................

Majority of women particularly in Indian context have agreed to customary terms and conditions prepared by society. But here Kamala Das has launched a war to give voice and arm to the millions of crushed women. "The ideal populace for a totalitarian state is faceless, voiceless one that will carry order without murmur."[38]

In the culture, creed and custom loaded state of India Kamala Das in the fashion of Anna Akhmatova wants to add face, voice, meaning and substance to the women's life. The poems analysed in the chapter "Veiled Beauty" have been composed within year 1955 - 60. A period popularly known for theoretic influence of Mahatma Gandhi which has been overthrown by Nehruism very soon. The decade of fifties is known for political honeymoon as India's administration was handed over to Eurocentric shrewd Indian politicians. Gandhian vision of India for future was almost trampled underfeet the very day Nehru took over as first prime minister of free India. Physically Mahatma Gandhi was assassinated by a freak called Nathu Ram Godse but spirit of Gandhism was dried out by those who took, maximum advantage of it. India as true Indian soil leaders dreamt and visualized of has scope of equality, fraternity, brotherhood, peace, prosperity and self - reliance for one and all. But the type of governance Nehru era gave was prone to corruption, inequality, nepotism, regionalism, ethnicism. As a result India instead of registering spectacular growth, got fragmented and mismanaged.

Kamala Das a sensible and thoughtful women of 25 years age then was unsatisfied with social, political and economic fragmentation of nation affecting the life of millions of papulance adversally. A poet like Kamala Das records the influence of prime national activity on the life of grassroots level men and women. The entire nation has been hopeful of high dreams coming to reality from independence but what happened afterwards was disparaging and gloomy. Hunger, poverty, illiteracy, disease, feticide, political - rivalry, nexus of crime, politics and beaurocracy infected the complete structures of country. Of these happenings Kamala Das had never been expectant. She became melancholy of prevailing evils in the society. In the all-round tempest of man - made evils most vulnerable victim have been women. Whatever social and political platform they avail they are very easily tarnished and victimized.

Along with national phenomenon there were several global events causing the kind of poetry Kamala Das wrote. Major global event include the end of European imperialism with the freedom of Indian in the year 1947. Soon after Indian freedom an anti-colonialism movement surged all over the world consequently many African, Australian and Latin American countries got liberty from colonizing nations. In feminist phraseology women's body has been colonial property of men, ceaselessly struggling for their salvation from patriarchy. Their movement got stimulus with the end of colonial rule. Very soon they sharpened their war at different stages from home to high political platforms, from poetry to journalism so on and forth. The Kamala Das kind of poetry is a reaction and outcome of worldwide women's struggle against exploitation of all sorts. Various organizations, platforms and self help groups were constituted everywhere to counter anti feminist stands. By their won endeavours women registered their presence in literature, science, administration, politics, social - work, sports, film, fashion and media. The stagnant male society was bound to admit down headed the feminist achievement. The period ranging from 1951 - 60 from feminist point of view is a period of realization whether traditional "Veil" on the face of beauty is worth maintaining? Many stances came in the life of womenfolk that they were deprived of basic amenities and esteem simply because of Veil. It was noway protector or enhancer of women's beauty but a barrier in the way of progress hence urgent removal of the same was felt necessary by Kamala Das. It hampers their access to the world of knowledge, shuns opportunity to understand the common deceptive world around fabricated by men. The notion of "Veiled beauty" is a deceitful slogan having in genuine colour of eulogy which Kamala Das does not withstand.

1. Mina Surjeet Singh, *Six Women Poets.* (New Delhi Prestige Publication, 2003), p. 105.
2. Manju Jaidka, *Recent Trends in Woman's Poetry,* (foreword), Prestige, New Delhi, p. 7
3. Z.F. Move, *Kamala Das: Homeless in the City,* (Critical Spectrum). p. 85.
4. *Ibid,* p. 92.
5. *Ibid,* (The Irony of Sex), p. 135.
6. Manju Jaidka, *Recent Trends in Woman's Poetry,* (Imperialist Design and Gender wars), p. 63
7. Kamala Das, *My Story,* (Sterling Publication, New Delhi), p. 5.
8. N.V. Raveendra, *Aesthetics of Sensuality,* (Intro. by K. Ayyappa Panicker), p. 33.
9. Jane Freedman, Feminism, (Viva Books: New Delhi),p. 26.
10. Manju Jaidka, *Recent Trends in Woman's Poetry,* p. 69.
11. *Ibid* (Poetry in The Times of Terror: Anna Akhmatova). p. 100.
12. A.N. Dwivedi, *Kamala Das and Her Poetry.* (New Delhi, Atlantic), p. 1.
13. *Ibid,* Pp. 2-3.
14. *Ibid,* p. 81.
15. Manju Jaidka, *Recent Trends in Woman's Poetry,* (Imperialist Design and Gender wars: Atwoods Power Politics), p. 47.
16. Kamala Das *My Story* A Poet at the Hustings, p. 169.
17. A.N. Dwivedi, *Kamala Das and Her Poetry.* p. 81
18. *Ibid,* p. 51.

19. Linda Hutcheon, *The Politics of Postmodernism*, (London: Routledge Fransus Group.) pp. 140, 141.
20. Leela Gandhi, *Post Colonial Theory* (New Delhi: OUP), p. 89.
21. A.N. Dwivedi, *Kamala Das and Her Poetry*. p. 73.
22. *Ibid*, p. 20.
23. Meena Alexander, *Women in Romanticism* (New Delhi-orient Longman). p. 1.
24. R. Mittapalli & Pier Paolo Picincco, *K.Das: A Critical Spectrum* (eds). p. 22.
25. Jai Kishna Nair, *The Onset of Poetic Rebellion*.............p. 65.
26. Z.F. Molvi, *Kamala Das: Homeless in the City*, (Critical Spectrum), p. 95.
27. *Ibid*, P,92.
28. *Ibid*, Sharda Iyer, *Self-Split in Kamala Das*, p. 117.
29. Manju Jaidka, *Recent Trends in Woman's Poetry*, (Writing Body: Anne Sexton), p. 43.
30. Kamala Das, *My Story* (New Delhi: Sterling Pub.), p. 35.
31. *Kamala Das and her Poetry*, p. 29.
32. *Ibid*, p. 22.
33. *Ibid*,p. 25.
34. Jane Freedman, Feminism (New Delhi: Viva Book), p. 26.
35. *Ibid*, p. 21.
36. *Ibid*, p. 22.
37. Manju Jaidka, *Recent Trends in Woman's Poetry* (Poetry in the Tine of Terror: Anna Akhmatova), p. 109.

3

Beauty at War

Darwinian theory of "survival of the fittest" applies most pertinently with life of women who right form the start of the human civilization have been fighting against anti forces. The war they kept going until now has been multi-layered and multi-faceted. The masculine strategy against feminine welfare has been also multi-dimensional sometimes apparent on surface and at other invisible and deceptive. The war of existence and identity is often cryptic in nature making it hard to manage in the favour of diseased. Since the dawn of civilization by way of religion and theology better - half has been put on the margin of existence not letting her know the mainstream activities of populace. The pioneer scriptures: Vedas, Bible, Quran, etc. have offered biased interpretation of women's existential reality. The Hindu scriptures and mythology present very mysterious and derogatory kind of pictures of women as the gateway to hell, illusion (Maya) and bone of contention. The Bible's stand on feminism is even more despicable that they are made of left out bones male as body. That women is a 'thing' of joy and consumption totally on the disposal of all governing man. Shakespeare's view of women manifest in Hamlet 'frailty thy name is women' is cause of feminist fury today. Tennyson's verdict that 'she is for hearth and needle and he for sword and battle' has proved futile and noway feasible in globalizing feminist welfare. Islam goes farthest in undermining the identity and value of women. They are treated in Islamic world as 'delicious delicacy' fit for brave Islamists slaying non-Islamists.

So called classic literature of different theological sects have similar notion of womanhood as they flourish from respective religion and mythology. The sense of 'time' and 'timelessness' is very crucial in making of ever valuable literature, this is what Kamala Das did in her writing. The place and position women enjoy today in every sphere of life is result of removal of Veil and engagement is existential war of survival. Had they not understood the deceiving tone of patriarchy they would have been 'used' in luxurious court of lusty kings as material of enjoyment. Kamala Das having under stood limitations of veil and fake aesthetics attached to corporeality of women has started paving quite new path of independence, individuality and self-assertion. The poems studied in this chapter have element of discontentment and disillusionment form the cheating path of patriarchy. At this stage she has raised war against any kind of women's exploitation by any individual or man-made institutions.

The very first poem chosen to analyze is "Radha" has mythological and contemporary significance. Radha is a kind of women who underscores unlimited love which has flown out for lord Krishna who in return offers the love that very way. The central thesis of the poem and that of love is this philosophy according to Kamala Das which is spontaneous reciprocation between Radha - Krishna. Dedication of one side is half of the circle producing no desirable result. In Hindu mythological and philosophical system the concept of 'ardhanareeswar' underlines the value of male and female who can perpetuate the cycle of nature, therefore it is necessary form the nature and social point of view to get them biologically and existentially united. Any kind of incongruity between male and female hampers the social system. Radha, as Kamala Das visualizes is representation of that nature element of fertility which animates and empowers Lord Krishna and vice - versa. She can wait for her timeless lover

(Krishna) indefinitely and hopes for certain of his arrival at her place. The calm and eternal river of love does not understand "doubting and the reasoning." Kamala Das's own life-story tells that she made unconditional love but found in result only dejection, hatred and lose of identity. For this and many other similar reasons she altered her paradigm to mythological characters like Radha and Krishna. In this matter N.V. Raveendran's remark is worth quoting, "In traditional Indian poetry treating Krishna myth, sexual union of Radha and Krishna is metaphorical; it signifies the union of "Prakrity" and "Purush". In Kamala Das's hand Radha and Krishna are loves but she does not garb them with the vestment of Bhakti. Her concern is not religious it is existential and literary."[1] According to my observation Kamala Das wants to apply Radha in current context as basic parameter of physical and emotional aesthetics. No relationship especially of man and women can last long unless and until either sides have admittedly imbibed the value of other. This is what Radha and Krishna did for each other and Kamala Das wishes to include in her professed agenda of post-modern women. What is occurring globally in connection with women is one sided, selfish and prejudiced. Even today in Indian social practices women open their flawless bosom to men resultantly finding only hurt and insult therein. The poem reveals transparent nature of Radha and today's feminist attitude:

> So that in his first true embrace she was girl
> And virgin crying
> Every thing in me
> Is melting even the hardness at the core
> O Krishna, I am melting, melting, melting
> Nothing remains but
> You.

"................a baseline definition of a common basic of all feminism" argues Jane Freedman, "may start with the assertion that feminism concerns themselves with women's inferior position in society ...."[2] But what Kamala Das advances by the character and unity of Radha - Krishna deserves deep feminist value. From outside advocacy favouring feminism is lesser in value than concrete understandable example of Indian myth of Radha - Krishna. The poem that follows "Radha" in an epitome of splitting and mismatching relationship between commercialized context of man and women - "The End of the Spring." The springful relationship of Radha - Krishna has got transversed into Eliot's *The Wasteland*. Kamala Das recalls the same in the following lines:

> I do not
> Know who to believe, you who say you love
> Or the voice that tells me no, no, no............
> Split each minutes into strangers, a lot
> Of them, a sort of game to fill the void
> In time, and avoid owning up to old deceit.

In the place of charactoral integrity postmodern man suffers the pangs of personality fragmentation manifest in the lines "You love ....the voice tells no, no, no." Kamala Das pin pointedly inspects the voice modulation containing at times element of love and no-.love while conversing on telephone. The lover's infringement of 'love' and undercurrent of mind telling 'no-love' is an instance of personality divisions. In the love affairs man plays crooked game with sincere beloved that is 'deceit' in plain terminology. In the atmosphere of 'deceit' 'fraud' and infidelity' how spring of love can bloom, laments Kamala Das. The entire surrounding is gloomy because of lack of genuine love between lovers and beloved that is compared with, "the street outside is dark and moist/ like limbs of sleeping girls." The dark and moist street" are neglected side of a city as "sleeping girls" are in society. In the life of Kamala Das as a neglected girl dwells moist darkness and melancholy. Things remain same, only tone of time changes as sunlight brings life to street and absence of that causes darkness to prevail thereon. Same cycle of light and dark comes and goes in the life of

Kamala Das. The poem projects the mercurial nature of life which changes from bright shade to dark. Arrival of death is identified with the arrival of night. The poet's obsession with darkness and death is very much close to Sylvia Plath's:

> I journey while alone just
> Backwards, taking secret steps inwards and
> Choosing roads none has walked before. My fear
> Is the fear of change; re-assuring me,
> As you do so often, does not help, for
> Even blood gets a colour-change, exposed.

As everybody feels that change is the nature of human life so Kamala Das is no mood of welcome to it, as it brings uncertain fear. The feminist change is always prone to tragedy because identity of women is always dependent on colonizing male argues Gilligan a noted feminist activist. She argues, "women saw themselves as connected to others as dependent others for their identity rather than autonomous and separate as men tend to see themself."[3] Death and tragic change haunt the life of women as it is monitored by archenemy. The entire system of society is governed and steered by phallocentric mentality which uses social customs as an instrument of women's exploitation. Kamala Das mourns women's lot because they are stereotyped and trained not to interrogate anti-feminist surroundings. "The spring dehydrating like a grape, meek/ Cow - smells on the breath of wind ——— ——what is the use / of love all this love if all it gives is fear." Love and hate for Kamala Das is almost identical as it gives no distinct feeling but fear. She has lost the sense of spring and delight coming from the intimacy of lover. The observation of Kamala Das about oppressed women community and that of Witting is almost similar, "women are nothing more than an oppressed social class."[4]

The domination, exploitation and torturing of women by the so-called lover / husband lead to eradication of identity and existence. These all amount to "The Suicide" the basic feature of women's personality. The timid, voiceless and non

- assertive nature of women are widely liked by male folk as these traits do not pose any challenge to exploitative strategies. Kamala Das wants to re-teach women of their strength and capability misused so far. The poem "The Suicide" discuses value and potentiality of "soul" often uncared in women's life. Body and soul are totality of existence which men never allowed women to realize. Male paradigm concentrates on feminist body as an object of possession. In the poetry of Kamala Das the image of "sea" recurs in different context. It denotes 'freedom', 'dominance', 'mental unrest' but here prejudiced male attitude. The body women wear is a colony of men and the 'soul' is most often uncared of by the two. Kamala Das concentrates on equal merit of body and soul like Robert Browning as the foundation of existence and aesthetic assertion refusing that is man - fabricated. She clarifies her view :

> I throw the bodies out,
> I cannot stand their smell
> Only the souls may enter
> The vortex of the sea.

The will-power can change negative atmosphere into positive maintains Kamala Das. By the magic of body the women cannot win the long defeated battle of life. She underscores all embracing nature of women's soul, "only the souls know how to sing / At the vortex of sea". What masculine force can do, even better and larger things women can do. French philosopher Simone de Beauvoir contends, "one is not born a women : one becomes one : escapitulates that women's inferior position is not 'natural' or biological' fact but that is created by society."[5] Women are incessantly trained to feel inferior before men as their biology is feeble and fragile.

> I throw the bodies out
> I cannot stand their smell
> Only the souls may enter

> The vortex of the sea.
> Only the souls know how to sing
> At the vortex of the sea.

There is confrontation and harmonization of body, soul and sea. The body does not carry any meaning unless attached to soul. Body is a poor thing as Kamala Das says "Dead as Driftwood, drifting / And drifting to the sea." Mighty sea can wallow up dead body unless it is coupled with soul. Soul is the centre of energy for body that seems absconding from the life of women hold Kamala Das. In this poem Kamala Das frequently uses 'body' in different situations denoting lack of strength but that does not belittle the value of it. The poem at this stage contains seed of struggle against all sorts of authoritism that has grown defunct with the passage of time. Man - Woman unity as the eternal foundation of society should be realized on terms of equality and co-existence rather than one ruler and other ruled. This attitude has been logically and powerfully countered by Kamala Das as Mary Erulkar records "the better service of womanhood is by Kamala Das."[6] Her historic service to womenfolk contains genuine element of fresh aestheticism which Radha - Krishna myth told centuries back. Flow of love on equal plain is more springful than one as higher giver and the other as wretched receiver.

The existential dilemma Shakespeare's Hamlet once confronted is repeatedly undergone by every woman on earth till date. The problem of 'to be or not to be' always haunts the protagonists Kamala Das created in her own image. In the system of nature women hold central position as the notion of 'ardhnareeswar' propounds but physical strength of man nurtured by women made her marginal and deprived comments Kamala Das.:

> I have enough courage to die,
> But not enough.
> Not enough to disobey him
> Who said, do not die

And hurt me that certain way.

Her own comparison with sea's roar and repetitive monotony is proper projection of feminist standpoint ever on recession. :

How easy our duties are.
How simple.
Only roar a hungry roar
Leap forward
And retreat.
You swing and you swing
O sea you play a child's game.
But,
I must pose
I must pretend
I must act the role
Happy wife.

Pretension, of high position and show off of what does not exist in reality are the typical life colours of Indian women. The hypocritical and artificial life pattern have rendered Kamala Das's life full of boredom and nausea which she wants to substitute by simplicity, originality transparency and honesty for self and relations. She pours out her concern in following words, "I want to be simple I want to be loved / And if love is not to be had, / I want to be dead, just dead." Life of women devoid of love is equal to death asserts Kamala Das that is also the initial point of her aesthetic discourse. The image of roaring "sea" conveys the multiple meaning of male mentality. As the male mind responds in a mercurial way dealing with women which the author notices in these lines, "The sea's hostile cold.........../ The sea's inner chambers / Are all very warm." Cold and warm go hand in hand in the life of man as far as his relation with women is concerned. Whatever is the nature of man in relation to women she has "The only movement ....is certainly the swim." Kamala Das's affinitywith sea surrounding comes from her ancestral house in Malabar that enriches her poetic expressions in various ways. In built innocence of Kamala Das has often been driven out by social and domestic restrictions as the following lines reveal. "My grandmother cried, / Darling, you must stop this bathing now. / You are much too big to play / Naked in the pond." The "nakedness" of Kamala Das's immature body can be understood as a symbolic manifestation of purity and transparency she had been sustaining in her mind till domestic tragedy (marriage) seized her. Whatever be the condition Kamala Das never genuflects to colonizer's terms and condition of physical and existential survival. R.K. Srinivas Iyengar in nominal words tells the basic features of Kamala Das's poetic and individual characteristics. :

> Her (Kamala Das's) claim for autonomy really flown from the felt sovereignty of her own individual existence. She is sinner, she is saint; she is the beloved, she is the betrayed, she is always and uniquely herself. Her distastes for words notwithstanding, they grow upon her "like a leaves on a tree", that provide her almost with an alibi, for she has stretched her "two dimensional nudity on sheets of weeklies and monthlies .... a sad sacrifice."[7]

The sacrifices of women in different roles have not be accounted for rather their "two dimensional nudity on monthlies and weeklies" have called hungry attention of man community, sarcastically comments Kamala Das. According to Indian heresies women's are attributed as illusion and ignorance entering the life of men which the author converts here by stating :

> Holding you is easy
> Clutching at moving water
> I tell you, sea
> This is easy,
> But to hold him for half a day
> Was a difficult task.

The poet's experience of her husband has been nasty and gloomy. She is bound to call her life "flop" and "bore" because her natural counterpart has beguiled her at every crucial stage. The final verdict of the author about her marital relationship is both tragic and challenging. :

> Lights are moving on the shore
> But I shall not return.
> Sea, toss my body back
> That he knew how to love
> ....
> My soul shall be free
> ....
> Only soul knows how to sing
> At the vortex of the sea.

The body - soul controversy clarifies that for a poet like Kamala Das soul is preferential entity as it provides her with larger scope of functioning. However body too has important place in terms of worldly affairs and assertion of identity. The second wave feminism (1960 onward) the period these poems she wrote had "protest again centered around women's inequality, though this time not only in terms of women's lack of political rights but in the areas of family, sexuality and work."[8]

The problem ridden life of women has been ever a central issue of Kamala Das's poetic expression be it sexuality, health, education or marginalization by patriarchy. Life of marginalized women struggles a lot to achieve centrality but as Kamala Das states in "Ferns" that "a time will come when / One of us will cry, candles burn no more / At both ends........" Metaphysical poet John Donne has used "taper" as metaphor for women's life burning on both ends. Beloved's scarifies does not deserve appreciative cognizance on the part of lover. Kamala Das as an advocate of feminist cause in India is in no mood of compromise with male dominated social and domestic ethics. Now she along with millions of women is on "run" to a new horizon of freedom, assertion and self esteem when arch enemies have no room of intervention. The beloved (candle) serves the purpose of light in the life of all but what she is awarded with is :

> ....where human sounds
> Never echoed, seas that which the craggy
> Shores and mountains where darkness grows.

The "darkness' covers inner and outer sphere of male society because of confined mindset. Love does not know high and love, poor or rich but flows on equal terrain of co-existence and mutuality. Kamala Das's her own physical and mental agony have universal implication as Arlene R.K. Zide observes, "......................that Kamala Das's themes transcends the 'personal' because what she attempts to poeticize is the universal experience of women."[9] The growth of "ferns" in dark and marshy corner of cold mountain is ironical in a sense, vibrant and energetic response of women which society has been finding till date is likely to exhaust because of universal negligence. And she further argues that "................a time will come / When words, while uttered, will fall thudding down / Like dismembered heads............." The atmosphere of love will deliberately get finished for ever. The love will not remain guiding and inspiring force in the life of society but an outcast sitting in isolation, ".............love will ride damp / Night - streets grinning in static mirth and at / Quite places eat its own hottest flesh................"

The thesis this poem advances is that meaning and vitality of love lives in both side response in identical manner barring which love is ritualistic and showy. See, again what Kamala Das maintains of static and normative love, "Bodies stacked on beds will mimick the slow / Gestures of the mind and take on the blame / In silent sin." Dead and formalistic entanglement of male - female body yields no spontaneity of love. In majority of matrimonial relations as G.B. Shaw also maintains only bodies respond and sprit escapes. In every poem she passes her female protagonist from one sad experience to another sadder so that she could transform her mind and body to cope well with male onslaught. Anishur Rehman claims that "images in Kamala Das's poems undergo metamorphosis and become symbols giving strength and vigour to her poetry." [10]

This kind of Kamala Das's warring and uncompromising attitude prepares for her a fertile ground of new feminist aesthetics. She declares as a wounded woman, "Escape now from such bonds / And from the precious staleness that we drag / From one country to another." No country, clime or community is conducive for proper growth and development of women as per the plan of the poet. They are strategically put on "Wait" mode for indefinite period. In an ironical manner she declares "............willing arms are thrust with / A sigh and "I've waited so long for you." This classic wait never meets with fulfillment, and the eyes of the waiting beloved get pertified.

Many poems of Kamala Das move same as the movements of the sea waves denoting the monotonous life of love. The poem "The Seashore" ends with a phrase. "And feel the loss of love I never once received." Which is main motif of women's life. The present poem "The Seashore" is indicator of gloom, dryness, lovelessness, and lack of self - esteem which all have been permeating the feminist space from the time immemorial past. There is a bunch of images denoting negativism as the main feature of womanhood, "The cremation ground", "Crunch of bones", "Vulgar mouth of fires" and "the smoke" and collectively create a background which every women inherit since birth. The atmosphere of negativity dominates in the following lines too, "Slowly stretch and rise, like serpents, satiated." The women's existence in the present social and domestic system is solely dependent on man's attitude, who is "a serpent satiated." The behavior of a satiated serpent cannot be unbiting. What men expect of women is her "body" falsely called love, the point Kamala Das debates as follows:

> give me time, more time and i

Shall learn to love. How often i
Wish, while you rest
In my arms and I could give you time that this
Great. All enveloping thing I offer you.

The phrase "all enveloping thing I offer you" involve physical and mental torturing. In the entire writing of Kamala Das recurring theme is "body" and "Love" emerging between man and women which she never romanticized nor glamorized. She "conveys here the power that a woman holds and her idiom is fundamentally modernistic (rather post - modernistic and realistic) instead of being romantic or idealistic or in the previous age."[11] In a sense Kamala Das in an author of 'presence' which runs for ever on the face of which drama of life is played in different hues. Everybody understands Kamala Das's marital life was an utter failure which she often confesses open heartedly. The dark patches of married life frequently haunt almost every poem evidently or cryptically. The following lines reveal unharmonious relationship between spouses especially exposes Kamala Das's married life:

..........All those destroying ones who
Leave you by
By night, to lie so ravaged
So spent like a sea shore
In empty hours under moon..........?

The husband seeking carnal satisfaction outside family and hoping wife to be fidel and chaste has no moral right to criticize the wife. The developing rift between husband and wife leads to absolute collapse of conjugal domestic and social fabric the pivotal idea on which the present poem is woven. Kamala Das a sensitive investigator of soft corners of women has every reason not to compromise with male mindset as it does not tolerate women's aesthetic development and individual existence.

The idea conveyed in "A phone call in the Morning" is

an attempt to bridge the gap between good states of mind to that of better by hoping a nice phone call in the morning. The element of romanticism unknowingly creeps in the poetry of Kamala Das not as a platform of rejoice but as a rejuvenator to struggling author. The third person expected to make a phone call between "you" and "I" is an old connection of author. She eagerly waits for the phone call but in the presence of husband says, "Those that spoke those very word / perhaps and after years let them die." Critics and general readers can understand that Kamala Das is an avowed author of woman's body. "not this body / now slightly worn that was both the players and the toy not this /hunger to set mouth to mouth and limb to limb— — —." The limb to limb contact in sexual relationship and the ecstasy emerging thereof in an outdated experience. It has gone in most matrimonial cases ritualistic and not a true emotion emerging from depth of existence condemns Kamala Das. The wedlock is a socio-ritualistic phenomenon and threads of love absolutely individualistic based on emotional understanding of the partners. Copulation is not love but playing with body-toy. The author reflects further on nature "but only the blue morning-dew-drenched/ bruised with bird sounds and the lawn." A.N. Dwivedi held that, "she is a poetess of love and sex and the body. — — — — "the human body" she celebrates it like the American poet Walt Whitman and regards it as a gift of God to human race."[12]

The Victorian poet Robert Browning celebrates human body in many ways as an evident mode of love making that convention in a more refined way Kamala Das also follows in a small poem "Love". The love is not a "doing" as male mindset maintains but a "happening" in between the two. Once the love has happened mind, personality emotion and existence of the lovers go enlarged spontaneously. But what happened with author is:

> Now that I love you,
> Curled like an old mongrel
> My life lies, content
> In you.

The word "content" is not used in positive sense rather, it is a dog like content that comes after feeding the belly and having the sex for her lover or husband. Kamala Das wants to explain dark surroundings of women's life before and after marriage eradicating their full development of personality and aesthetic sensibility. The idea is further enlarged in the poem "In Love" which talks of misconceptions of popular love. The feeling of love is not fulfilled by having frequent sexual contacts with husband rather it entails a lot of things more. She compares burning sky with her body burning and the response of her husband is something like .... "his / mouth ....and his limbs like pale and carnivorous plants reaching out for me, and the sad lie of my unending lust." The feelings of "lust" and "love" are pole apart very often misunderstood. That point Kamala Das wants to bifurcate. In a case of genuine love even an embrace is a complete thing. Love making is a kind of jigsaw game which creates complex to more complex situation. Both partners of love game calculate their opportunity of victory over the other in terms of pleasure sharing. Contemporary British author Thom Gunn (1929 - 2003) describes love game in terms of war strategy. "Even in bed I pose." The tradition of John Donne seems getting repeated here by Kamala Das:

> When mouth on mouth,
> I lie, ignoring my poor
> Moody mind, while pleasure
> With deliberate gaiety
> Trumpets harshly into
> The silence of the room.

The image that follows is indicative of frustration and hopelessness likely to pervaid in the life of played upon object women. See the hovering dark scene of women's married life:

> At noon
> I watch the sleek crows flying

Like poison on wings and at
Night from behind the Burdwan - Road
The corpse - bearers cry Bol
Hari Bol .... I walk
The verandah, sleepless,
A million questions awake in me
All about him and this
Skin communicated thing

A logical question is here raised by author that what does "Love" mean in totality? It is skin communication or something wider, deeper, larger involving the personality, existence and esteem of women as a complete individual. What is superficial is not love but lust asserts the author. In the present domestic setup women are considered as "Convicts" the idea is traditionally validated by Bible, Quran, Vedas and even by William Shakespeare when he criticizes women by calling them "frailty thy name is women." The illogical notion of women which society promotes Kamala Das wants to refute by offering a wide and valid platform of thought process and aesthetic manifestation. The poem "Convicts" interprets the down position of women in every affair of life including sexual practices. She says, "our lusts were / Like multi - coloured flags of no particular country." The feeling of love knows neither gender nor climate to grow. It is a flag of feelings asserting it between the lovers's indiscriminately. The poet further asserts:

We lay
On bed, glassy eyed, fatigued, just
The toys dead children leave behind,

After having sexual orgy Kamala Das finds herself emotionally and physically tottered like a dead toy left over by negligent boys. The kind of love women encounter in routine is discontentment enlarged because of mere physical contact. "That was the only kind of love, / this hacking at each other's parts / like convicts." How a healthy relationship can grow when women are conditioned to realize her birth as sin? No attempt of woman has produced positive consequence on the mind of man regarding woman's value. From religion to politics and home to street women are looked upon as an object of luxury fit for consumption afterwards likely to be discarded. This state of matter is plight feels the author in the following lines :

> There was a burning in our veins
> ....
> When he and I were one
> We were neither male nor female.
> There were no words left, all words
> Lay imprisoned in the ageing
> Arms of night.

The moments of conjugal intimacy erase the distinction of male and female identity by elating them to the level of unspeakable enjoyment. This kind of harmony and emotional understanding Kamala Das wants to build for entire society which male partners deliberately damage by egocentric impositions. There are many examples where feminist contributions have been not only overlooked but trampled under feet. Who can deny the share of Judith Shakespeare in William Shakespeare and that of Dorothy in William Wordsworth, perhaps this in one of the reasons Virginia Woolf challenges the validity and authenticity of literary history by asserting "re-write the history". Meena Alexander reads feminist writing through a totally, different paradigm. "Beneath the embattled surface of women's writing, lay a less obstrusive search : for a new forms of literary knowledge, for a territory shaped by the truth of a female life."[13] Kamala Das has not borrowed any thing for her writing from theory or day - dreaming. It all is fruit of her body and mind felt practical experiences. In "Convicts" the author perceives harmony and beauty of nature spread everywhere as the model to follow up in domestic life of married couples:

In darkness we grew as in silence
We sang, each note rising out of
Sea, out of wind, out of earth and
Out of each sad night like an ache

The entire natural elements are eternally tagged to each other forming a composite system of universe, we (the male and female) being part of this cosmic system do not follow that natural harmony and beauty in our domestic matters. Disobeyance to natural order leads to universal and individual desperation and dissonance visible in every sphere of life which Kamala Das wants to uproot by substituting harmony, rhythm, and love.

Religious, social and ethical conviction train women to adhere to patriarchal morality. The issue is debated in "Loud Posters" a poem that allows Kamala Das to be frank, open and obscene to some extent that challenges centuries old morality. The kind of openness she has in her writing is not available in other contemporary feminist authors says Parthsarthy. The poempresently under analysis "Loud Poster" is a testimony of post modern women's biting response to male onslaught. The very opening line of the poem foreshadows what she is going to do in future:

I am today a creature turned inside
Out. To sread myself across wide highways
Of your thoughts, stranger, like a Loud poster,
Was my desire.

The suppressed desires of man and women have been to enlarge their identity across the world. In this attempt man succeeded and women failed. But today with the reversal of situation women are assertive of their body, mind and caliber. So far they have been strategically narrowed upto skin beauty. But today as Kamala Das declares :

I have stretched my two dimensional
Nudity on sheets of weeklies, monthlies,

Quarterlies, a sad sacrifice. I have put
My private voice away, adopted
The type writers click as my only speech.

The concept of house bound, beautified husband caring and sex offering women is no longer available in the territory of women. They are in the mood of decisive war against any kind of exploitation and aggression that women have been suffering. The presentation of "two dimensional nudity" on weeklies is a timely reaction to male-gaze, Kamala Das accepts that in case of war and love every posture stands fair. Linda Hutcheon argues in *The Politics of Postmodernism* that "Traditionally the representation of the female body has been the province of men. Except in advertising, perhaps women are not usually intended addresses of pictures of women."[14] The consented presentation of feminist nudity, argues Kamala Das is for greedy male gaze and to feel defeated because of the subtle body magic of women is not final. Since her body and life have been a battle always won by man is currently turned opposite. By hook or by crook they have finalized to stand victorious in ancient battle of both genders. The argument of Linda goes on, "..........................the body of women when used by men is colonized, appropriated, even mystified, when used by women that body reveals, its fertility, self sufficient sexuality"[15] and self esteem.

The controversy that entails women's life very often is body mystery. The complete life women devoted for others sacrificing her selfhood is precisely declared null and void by natural counterpart. The poet in very appropriate, terminology suggests women's life annals as "Someone Else's Song". She is nowhere in her own life rather husband, son, relatives and someone else occupy central place in her life. The central phrases of the poem very objectively tell what women's sum of life stands for? See the focused statement of Kamala Das :

I am a million million people

I am a million million deaths
....
I am a million million births
....
I am a million million silences. ....

The first word "people" denote crowd like identity of women having no distinctive feature of their own. Death is a natural event following which comes mourning rendering women's life monotonous. The most important verb "birth" indicates women's uncelebrated state of life. Nothing remains in the life of unmourned "death" and uncelebrated "birth" of women except reluctant "silences". The "silence" permeating life of women is neither spiritual silence nor meditational but silence of mortuary. They can not have schooling, healthcare or can have any "say" in the domestic affairs. Their pains are almost voiceless as no ardent listner or sympathizer is all around. The state of being "voiceless" yet singing the song of others is (men's) an unspeakably paradoxical. Undergoing the pangs of others on the cost of selfhood is how painful only a woman can understand. Meena Alexander has rightly remarked that women's contribution in the life of males considerable yet on the part of male they are ever undervalued, "obviously it is impossible to put into a poem, novel or journal actual and substantial bits of one's physicality into the text."[16] The "other" always stands "other", who cannot know painful internal truth a woman happens to confront in different context of life. The smallest unit of society is family constituted of multiple relationships of mother father, husband and wife etc. The present poem "The Snobs" offers a very dark picture of weakening relationships resulting into familial and individual dissociation. The opening line "Our houses crouches in dust" is a symbolic manifestation of disintegrating domestic fabric. The Indian countryside was free from city bred evils but post independence development corrupted the entire system down to the root. The images of "buffaloes stramp up the road", "the weary herdsmen singing soft-Punjabi song" and "girls from free Municipal school" suggest the grass root level reality of rural India. Despite poverty and lack of bookish education these people have love for children and honour and care for elderly people. Presenting herself as a representative of city manners Kamala Das open heartedly says, "What have I to offer them but / my smile, a half dead fraudulent thing. What I have to offer at / this shrine of peace but my constant / Complaining voice"?

The most valuable offer is smile and love that too we shrink because of computing temperament of city life. The transparent mood of Kamala Das utters:

> Forgive us. We are
> Paltry creatures, utter snobs
> Who disowned our mothers only because
> Their hands, we noticed, were
> Workworn and so to seek richer
> Mother's and better addresses ....

In the gamut of Kamala Das's writing mother image is almost indelible. Her career as a poet has got stimulus from mother's and grandmother's affectionate treatment. The contribution of mother in the making of children's personality positive and fertile Kamala Das esteems very high, for this and many other valid reasons she in the manner of Anglo-American feminist "calls for a total re-thinking, a re-visioning of a world, re-envisaging a new order where women will receive her due dignity and respect. Like the French feminist she focuses on her body visualizing its needs and desires as a special language, a medium which a woman may use to communicate her deepest thoughts her inner most feelings."[17]

The central message of the poem says that scientific law of action and re-action is equally applicable in the life of common man. Today we discard our elderly parents, tomorrow we will be disowned by our sons and grandsons. The chain of negative behavior should cease says Kamala Das by spreading loving and caring atmosphere this is what

Kamala Das wants to propagate as her principle of contemporary aesthetics. A woman like Kamala Das some times becomes freak because of unfriendly atmosphere creating boredom and suffocation. What her husband wants most often of her is "body" that is not "love". This contradiction compels Kamala Das to cry aloud like a freak. She does not conceal the private moments, "his right hand on / my knee while our minds willed to race towards / love only wander, tripling idly over / puddles of desire." Husband intends to colonize the body of woman (wife) whereas she wants emotional proximity then anything else. But physical strength of husband dominates the soft and finer feelings of wife. "According to Witting women are nothing more that oppressed social class."[18] The voice of oppressed class (women) goes ever unheard no matter it is valid, just and beneficial for individual and system.

The above thought is still perpetuated in the poem titled "The Descendants". The poem has two persons operating inside the structures of it: one Kamala Das and second her lover / husband whom she does not want to accept in the given domestic circumstances. Certain phrases prove the infidelity existing between the two, for example, "sinning exchanging insubstantial love" and "no pain could remain in us" and "no bruise could scar" and "cold loveliness" powerfully indicate unharmonious relationship between Kamala Das and her husband. Their wedlock is in the state of decay. Another set of imagery again paint unclicking relationship:

> While hours passed in a half dusk, half dawn
> And half dream, half real trance
> We were the yielder,
> Yielding ourselves to everything

The temple of marriage, maintains Kamala Das is as pious as God's but mal-practices of husband makes it dirty and filthy consequently the entire domestic network goes foul. Of an on the poet philosophizes the matrimonial matters like

John Donne because of her upbringing was done is a typical Nair family of Malabar. She argues:

> but as child to mother's arms
> we have given us to the fire or to
> the hungry earth to be slowly eaten,
> devoured.

In the poetry of Kamala Das earth fire, water, sky and wind the basic elements of body composition frequently appear in order to press the present physicality and unlitmate destination of body. What we make by our endeavours that that we use, neither God nor any other agent comes forward to assist us in the matters of personal relationships and otherwise. The concluding lines reveal the semi-philosophic attitude of Kamala Das:

> no God lost in
> silence shall begin to speak, no lost Love
> claims us, no, we are not going to be
> redeemed or made new.

According to Karma theory of Bhagwat Geeta we make and mar our selves by our noble or ignoble selves or by our noble or ignoble doings. Neither God nor any other superpower can be held responsible for making / marling the life of ours. The theory equally applies on husband-wife relationship. She refers to mythology of Radha-Krishna as an ideal stage of love flow where non in higher or lower:

> Kamala Das has turned Indian myths occasionally into symbolistic imagery and one such myth is Radha-Krishna syndrome. The myth assumes the shape of a recurrent symbol in her poetry. When she looks around and discovered a vast gap between the real world and the world of her dreams she became pessimistic in her outlook upon life and applies this myth as a symbol of her salvation.[19]

Salvation for Kamala Das is not freedom from life afflictions rather amicable understanding based on affection and co-existence. Creation of healthy atmosphere among family members, especially between husband and wife is the solo motive of Kamala Das. Whosoever intervenes her attempt she likes to kick out even from the memory arena. The above idea is well versed in "Lumino". She wants to sleep by ignoring intimate villain, "it is only / Wise to let sleep / make holes in memory", no matter the sleep is pill induced. Why Kamala Das prefers pills for sleep because "he shall not enter / Your ruthless one, / being human clumsy / with noise and movement, the soul's mute arena". She wants to keep soul's arena totally free of dissonant elements. There is always struggle in the poetry of Kamala Das against male attitude which creates commotion in the peaceful arena of women. In her *My story,* Kamala Das dismantles domestic unrest which was presumed to be harmonious outwardly, "mother has timidly created an illusion of domestic harmony and produced some half a dozen children of swarthy skin and ordinary features."[20] For production of children women's consent is not generally sought by the pregnating beast (husband). The husband punishes wife for life long by a sexual deed of momentary excitement which in view of Kamala Das is a sin unless emotional consent of better half is achieved.

The salient features of husband wife relationship is understandable in a new metaphor which "Palam" poem communicates. The pivotal phrase of this poem is "walk away from me into this lonely night." Whom the poet scolds to go away in dark night is none but her life-partner. It is identical to "Like blood running out and death beginning." The life of Palam aerodrome is because of aero planes landing with many passengers in it. As the plane has taken off the scene at Palam gives deserted look. "While plane drones on at the distance and the airport's lights gleam blue." In this poem Kamala Das has come across with a dilemma of expression. Some times her expression applies to aero plane and then to her lover towards whom she has a grudge. "Go deep into night, a victor as cold now as his blade, dark falcon, / late returning". The "falcon" and "victor" words definitely indicate the nature and behaviour of husband.

Since there is a long standing score between husband and wife therefore different derogatory metaphors Kamala Das uses to denote her position and that of husband's attitude. "The Maggots" is a very simple but suggestive poem revealing the unspoken pain of women. They are not only put on margin of socio domestic system but denied their natural right to live with honour. On the bank of river Yamuna Krishna used to love Radha without care and comment of society. In the embrace of husband Gopi felt almost lifeless because husband's embrace is carnal whereas Krishna's pure on scale of equality. She is victimized by social tradition of marriage. Her husband asks "do you mind my kisses. / and Love, she said, no not at all". The state of numbness and lifelessness is indicative of defunct marriage system wherein husband and wife are yoked by force of social and ritual systems. In fact, according to Kamala Das, the only condition of marriage is love and co-existence. The concept of equal love originally propounded by "Radha-Krishna" is the theme of the poem titled same. Love experience relates to soul and body. Kamala Das in matter of love adheres to the Browining tradition but being an Indian origin cannot deny the value of soul in love - discussion. The reference to Kadamba tree, river and Radha - Krishna physicality suggest the story of their's in a postmodern context. Interpretation of Radha-Krishna myth in the contemporary context is a unique socio-literary experiment observed by A.N. Dwivedi is worth recalling in this case, "It is this (Radha-Krishna or Mira-Krishna myth) framework that saves her in some degree from the charges of obscenity and promiscuity, otherwise her poetry is replete with shocking and orthodox details about love, marriage and sex."[21]

The debate of physicality and non-physicality as the base of love continues in the following poem "Vrindavan". The immediate response one gets from the word "Vrindavan" is the love-site of Radha-Krishna and nothing else. The charm of poem lies in the universalisation of "Vrindavan" as a feeling of love present in all women than a physical place to be seen only. Again Kamala Das disapproves normative kind of. love-bond. Despite being married to other man all Gopis would fly to Krishna flute discarding domestic and social ethics of marriage. Even more they show their breast bruises to husbands because of playing and dancing with Krishna on thorny bushes. This kind of love says Kamala Das brings meaning and harmony in conjugal relationship otherwise marriage is a social phenomenon sacrificing two stranger's individuality.

The lives of individuals (husband and wife) get destroyed on the altar of marriage only fulfilling the formalities of hollow social conventions and religious rituals. Kamala Das is consummate artist in transforming concrete images into emotional abstractions. The technique she applies in "Summer in Calcutta" is unique and wonderful in making Calcutta's weather as suffocating emotional experience. She drinks hot and humid weather of Calcutta squeezed by "April sun" like a orange juice in glass. The unpalatable juice she has been drinking all through life is bitterness of wedlock. "I sip the / fire / I drink and drink / again, I am drunk". The state of drunkenness does not refer to hilarious married life, rather it indicated to unavoidable perpetuality of afflictions. The irony of Kamala Das still goes on, "what noble / Venom flows through / my veins and fills my / mind with unhurried laughter"? Especially two words "noble venom" and "unhurried laughter" are sufficient parameter showing the flow of poisonous under current in the life of author. The idea is underscored in a very poetic manner the style resounds Sarojini Naidu's, "wee bubbles ring / my glass / like a pride's / nervous smile and meet my lips. Dear forgive / this moment's lull in wanting you."

Kamala Das has been always a fidel chaste and honest about her infatuation towards husband. It is husband who played betrayal with the deeper feelings of Kamala Das followed by revolt, wrath and total denial of marriage institution in its conventional form and content. No woman authors along with Kamala Das has dared to pinpoint the issues of aesthetics in such a subtle way. In west, "It was only with Dorothy Richardson, Katherine Masefield and Virginia Woolf that a deliberate 'female aesthetics' appeared."[21] This kind of pioneering job in Indian sub-continent was done by Kamala Das alone. Formation of aesthetic background by digging the hard-path of feminism in India Kamala Das is doing a historic job. Despite perpetual struggle there is possibility of defeat and genuflection as the poem indicates the idea powerfully. :

How brief the term of my
devotion, how brief
your rein when I with
glass in hand, drink, drink,
juice of April sun.

Frequent use of "drink" suggests conventional conditioning of women which they wish to alter by self-choice but April sun (metaphor for husband) furiously shines in sky increasing the plight of women. The life of women is always shadowed by male dominance even in strictly private affairs. The dark shadow under which feebly pulsates feminist life hungrily asks for "oh love me, love me, love me till I die................" but she gets no love but "death" is the theme of "Morning at Apollo Pier." The poem begins with a note of enthusiasm but abruptly comes to a deadlock. In Indian cultural tradition women are subject of high esteem in every matters pertaining to society and family. But doctrinal reality never came in the life of women even in smallest bits. The beauty of nature (particularly sea) has been a fascinating experience in the poetry of Kamala Das, which prepares a background of matrimonial reality, "beautiful men, / inadequately loved, walking to find a fatigue in their limbs".

Expectation of love by male is always one sided on the stupid logic of patriarchal dominance, whereas Kamala Das has faith in Radha - Krishna sort of love where no one is inferior to other. She offers a very disparaging scene :

> I saw
> The cripple stump along, hunger was both
> His crutch and his limb, I saw the jerky
> Walk of the very young.................

The series of description show how helpless and ineffective conjugal relation has grown because of behavioral frigidity. It is crippling, lifeless and confined up to sexuality that too for the momentary physical satisfaction of male partner. This kind of relationship produces boredom and mental inertia Kamala Das notes in the remarks of fellows:

> They tell me, all my friends, that I am finished,
> that I can write no more, they tell me
> that the goose which lays the golden eggs can lay
> no more, they tell me that your love is
> a morass where I must sink.

The creative barrenness Kamala Das also realizes all around but being a pioneer and feminist advocate she does not accept final defeat. Her war against phallocentric attitude is always alive till she is physically and mentally capable. In the concluding lines of the poem she utters:

> You are the poems to end all poems
> a poem, absolute as the tomb.
> Your flawed beauty is my only refuge
> Oh love me, love me love me till I die.

The struggle for women's cause she has to continue till her death. It is a mission, and meaning of Kamala Das's life to live and lay down life for women's welfare. Kamala Das an obsessed advocate of women community suffers the similar afflictions as her matrimonial bond is victim of mal - adjustment. She compares her physical identity as a "rag doll" which better adjusts with the sexual demands of husband. Husbandial attitude is very discarding as the first few lines reveal. "One sedatives / I am more lovable / says my husband." Having taken intoxicant her beauty of body and speech resemble "Heron" a bird known for alluring song and flight. How helplessly Kamala Das admits her inability to resist untimely lust of husband. "my rag doll limbs adjust to his versatile lust." The word "versatile" denotes wantonness of male lust which does not know clime, time or mood of the partner. This kind of sexual feudalism Kamala Das not only disapproves but wants to disengage herself from. The poem "Herons" is a representation of attitude clash between conservative line of society and postmodernist doctrine of author that results into a new path breaking for contemporary aesthetics a blend of physicality, love, understanding and co - existence on the parameter of equality.

What hampers the formation of new feminist aesthetic highway according to Kamala Das is not completely weeded out as their root is manured from the ancient time by religious and social mal practices. The theme of the poem "Weeds" is portrayal of that negative element which grows every where in a large quantity. The central phrases "faith grows but in silence" and "a woman's voice / sounds best in memory" have a lot to indicate for those who are able to read the undercurrents of husband-wife bonds. Relationship is not for verbal explanation but for inner understanding Kamala Das is tired of relational monotony, she wants to revive it on the plain of mutuality and understanding but "His gross face imprisons, / the right response. With strange words Whip lashed............." The feminist sensibility of Kamala Das is keener and deeper in understanding the mental ripples of husband's but his concealing of pains hurts her. "I let the weeks slide by and wait for silence to grow like / weeds among words once spoken." On the state of "silence" and misunderstood "spoken works" Kamala Das prefers to choose the first because the later creates confusion piled on confusion as T.S. Eliot comments on verbosity of modern man, "words among words unable to express a word." As a flag bearing author of twentieth century woman Kamala Das has yet a long way to move, "as we have noticed .... her poems explore not only the self but universal experience of the women. These explorations go beyond the limitations of feminism while exploring the problem of women her poems embrace the problem of humanity in general."[23] She is a seeker of truth entangled in known and unknown paradigms of human existence. It would be unfair to attribute Kamala Das the totem of feminist writer, in addition to that she is avowed humanist and advocate of equality among mankind.

She does not hesitate in criticizing Lord Krishna in the poem "Krishna" where she says "Your body is my prison" the word prison does not entail positive implication, rather it offers hatred and lack of trust in between the two. But in the same poem she transfers her "Prison" attitude to still deeper antipathy the world offers for women "Your love words shut out the wise world's din" hence your "Prison of body"is someway preferable. The idea the poem thus advances is that women's life always confronts two way dilemma; the inferior one being acceptable. The confined state of feminism in India is suffering various shackles the idea is poetically rendered by the poet, in The Prisoner. The prison stands for patriarchal mindset and prisoner is women and their grey shaded life. What assertion Kamala Das makes in the final lines of the poem is brief but bold agenda, "I must some day find / and escape fro its snare." Kamala Das wants to assert that women's life and body are not morsel of man's dish. She talks and declares her dignity as an individual in the stampede of male atrocities. Emily Dickinson an American poet was victim of male prejudice when she was composing her poems. "Emily Dickinson was also a victim of patriarchal conventions and so she hid her talent from public eye. So was the case with a number of other women writers who were either unaware of or the timid to break the patriarchal norms in which they were steeped."[24]

The following poem "Gino" is a large scale exposition of intimate moments of author in which she concludes her partner's attitude that is largely poisonous. "You will perish from his hiss" and "one must surely die when bitten by a krait that fills / the bloodstream with its accursed essence." The elaboration Kamala Das offers is a powerfully testimony of her bitter experiences. "I was quiet, / for once, my tongue had fainted in my mouth." The second scene presents an atmosphere of suffocation, boredom and rigidity symbolizing factual condition of women in four wall confinement of domesticity. :

> ....July full of rain and darkness
> Trapped like smoke, in the hollows of the sky, and
> That lewd, steamy smell of rot, rising out of earth.
> The west wind leaking
> ....
> Through his hair, and I thought
> If I could only want,
> Really truly want his love.... .

The feminist desire of love never appropriately get fulfilled as the lover is focused to body not to soul or personality. In the phraseology of Semon de Beuvoir women's body is an acient colony of man, Kamala Das also reiterates the same thing, "fair conquer of another's country." The game of "win and defeat" endlessly goes on in the life of man and woman. The impact of this rivalry never lets them live on the plain of trust, faith and fidelity. The life long discard Kamala Das has been confronting is equivalent to that of American feminist author Stevie Smith, "She (Stevie Smith) voices her protest against patriarchal order in a very subtle and civilized manner. There is a genteel quality about Smith's poetry which speaks volumes for the culture she was groomed in, the culture she knew she had to conform in order to survive in a world that was indifferent to women's aspirations."[25]

Kamala Das in "Gino" and elsewhere too wants to confirm the great Indian culture and domestic norms in her early volumes but while finding this process to be self-slaughtering she altered her stand to protest and aggression. The sexual activities of husband she recalls like "I dream of obscene hands / striding up my limbs and morgues where the night lights / glow on faces shuttered by the soul's exit." The body of husband and wife entangled in sexual orgy devoid of soul is a game of mechanical toys laments Kamala Das. Such kind of relationship can better be explained in the personal life experience of author when she was passing through different medical investigation. "(oh the clatter of the trolleys, with the dead on them, / as loud as untimely laughter.............)". The scene that follows intensifies the anguish the author has been feeling for long. "And of aeroplanes bursting red in the sky." Bursting red in sky is an image showing painful days of Kamala Das's life that is hard to erase. What Kamala Das's husband hopes of life is absolutely contrary to what she herself wants, :

> dreams of sunlit villas and fat
> half caste children lovelier that God's and of
> drinking wine in balconies, he and I ageing
> and at peace, all disguise gone from us.

Material requirement do not fulfill the imperfections of personality opines Kamala Das. She does not undervalue the human body rather she wishes to supplement "body" with "wisdom" of togetherness missing which life has gone to total absurdity. Remarkable are her lines in this case. :

> This body that I wear without joy this body
> burdened with lenience, slender toy owned
> by man of substance shall wither battling with his
> impersonal lust.

"Impersonal lust" that husband quenches by the aid, of wife is often sidelined in matter of honour and equal domestic and social status. She along with her individualities is marginalized to a dangerous degree, :

> I shall be the fat-kneed hag in the long bus queue
> the one from whose shopping -- bags the mean potato
> must
> roll across the street. I shall be the patient
> on the hospital - bed, lying in the drugged slumber
> and dreaming of home.................

The sum of woman's life is to kill her personality and existence on the altar of domesticity which finally signifies nothing. The idea can be better put in Shakespearian phrase "Life (of a woman) is a tale told by and idiot .... signifying nothing." In the concluding part she underscores feminist desire to enter again in the mother's dark womb with inherent protesting tendency so that the coming generation could be framed on women-friendly atmosphere. The concept of contemporary women's aesthetics, according to Kamala Das is where not only feminism prevails but humanism. She does not endorse injustice done even from the side of women. Her opinion is quit candid that for health of social and domestic relationship both natural participants must-honour each other. The poem "The Testing of the Sirens" describes the uneven social and domestic condition of women which Kamala Das raises for open front debate by all. Concealed and imposed concept of women's beauty does not satisfy the furious mind of author. The life of women as a toy in the hand of man is no way tolerable, for Kamala Das. The lover comes to beloved in the fall of the dark night. He is also "dark-cloaked like procuress." He is willing the beloved's love because it cannot be had in the market place. He, "Speaking words of love / in some tender language I do not know .... and my limbs / worm from love were once again so lonely ...." He offers alluring words of love for the beloved who unwillingly consented the proposal. The position of women in terms of relationship is very transitory having no substantial say. "I have / washed my face with soap and water, brushed my hair a dozen / times draped myself in six yards of printed / voile." These mechanical and lover oriented activity of woman show lack of individuality and personal choice tending to uproot her identity.

The main worry of author reflected in the present poem is woman's subordination to man preferred paraphernalia. Even apparels ornaments and beautification styles are not feminist rather chosen by men :

I said, what I can do for you? I smiled
A smile is such a detached thing. I wear
It like a flower, ...

Another chain of images showing commodification of women for the taste of man is presented in a very filthy and obscene way :

Near he take, a pregnant
Girl based her dusky
Breast and washed them sullenly. On the
Old common stand, crows bickered over a piece
Of lizard - meat.

Kamala Das creates different contrasting images and situation showing slippery stand of women in society. She is loved and liked for a specific purpose after which thrown away like a garbage. This sort of opportunistic attitude Kamala Das does not rectify and include in her draft of aesthetic ideology. In a famous study Women in Ancient India, S N Sinha and N K Basu advance a very valid argument about women's reality in society. :

> Many modern anthropologist and sociologist have proved not without reason that prostitution is an essential constituent of the whole marriage system as it appears today and was the indirect result of the gradual development of the family on patriarchal and mostly monogamic basis. It is for one to consider whether it may be accepted a premise with which to work the problem with any hope of success.[26]

Marriage in most societies is a kind of modified prostitution because woman's consent in this regard is sidelined. G.B. Shaw has shown greater concern for his female characters who represent down trodden condition of women. "The Dance of the Eunuchs" is a presentation of miseries under which not only eunuchs but all women some or the other way roll down. Being "female" in our society is equal to being nothing rather worse than eunuchs. It is a sarcastic comment on the mood and manners of society shown towards women in general. The mentality through which eunuchs are looked upon is not only insulting but antagonistic. Kamala Das has given a very pitiable picture of eunuchs and that of common man who do not consider them living creatures. The author's empathy runs from creatures to human beings, manifesting her range of humanistic observation." They danced and / They danced, oh they danced till they bled." Dance for eunuchs is not a passion but compulsion of livelihood earning that is not possible in the cut throat competitive world. Very objective picture that Kamala Das shows reveal outward factuality of eunuchs to attract people for some pieces of coin, :

> They were green
> Tattoos on their cheeks, jasmines in their hair, some
> Were dark, and some were almost fair. Their voices
> Were harsh, their songs melancholy; they sang of
> Lovers dying and of children unborn............

In the songs of eunuchs there is critical comments on unfair events of society which have taken deep root in conventions as "Lovers dying" and "Children (female) unborn." The dejected lot of society is eunuchs living on the last edge of system in terms of honour and position have deep penetrating observation. In the ecstasy o‘ :nce they "beat their sorry breasts" and some "writhea in vacant ecstasy." The phrase "vacant ecstasy" reveals the emotional vacuum in the life of these people at domestic and social level. They are treated as robots programmed to entertain people around. More melancholy facts Kamala Das presents in the following lines, :

> They
> Were thin in limbs and dry, like half burnt logs from
> Funeral pyres, a drought and rottenness
> Were in each of them.

....

All were watching these poor creatures' convulsion

The eunuchs were not only dancing but passing through physical convulsion that basically originates from mind. "Half burnt logs from funeral pyres", "drought and rottenness" and "urine of lizards and mice" bring out tragic reality of these people's life. The other facts of life which Kamala Das wants to hint at is immoral and in human attitude of common society towards them.

The rotten and burnt logs are like life of women and eunuchs have instigated Kamala Das to strengthen her mission against male-psychology. She utters her anger in "A Request" which exposes how reactive and stubborn attitude she possesses against patriarchy, :

When I die
Do not throw
The meat and bones away
But pile them up
And let them tell
By their smell
What life was worth
On this earth
What love was worth
In the end.

The reaction towards patriarchy is very sharp and repulsive. Kamala Das has very uncompromising attitude in the matters of familial relationship. She wants her flesh and bones be piled to show how much humiliation and mistrust women used to have since the dawn of civilization. The perfection of a woman's life lies in becoming a mother of a son. Ironically the very son becomes the conventional enemy of womenfolk. The idea is well incorporated in the poem "Jaysurya" the name of the author's son. The poem advances its argument in systematic natural images showing various developmental stages in nature. When Kamala Das has

Jaisurya born it was time of heavy rain and trees were weeping. The author creates a scene of stage of life reflecting anguish of woman and underlying contradiction. After rain the "moss" appeared on earth as "eczema" on woman's body, the paradoxes still continue, "beneath the swashy earth / the fat worms surfaced / to explode under rain." The mother is symbolized by "earth" as the originator of greenery, moss and worms on its body which all explode the body of earth as son does with mother. Very symbolic presentation is offered by the rainfall as delivery of her son to be largely identical in present and future implications. :

> It rain rained on the day my son was born.
> a slanting rain that began
> with the first labour pain and
> kept me company
> sighing, wailing and
> roaring when I groaned
> so that I stopped my plaits
> to hear its griefs.

The pain of labouring mother Kamala Das and that of rain is almost equivalent in terms of circumstantial response. General opinion about pain is that "selfish had fears that unloving felt pain." Both mother and nature have unselfish and caring temperament yet they undergo largest degree of pain. A tinge of blood seen at the moment of labour pain Kamala Das takes as "another dawn breaking." But very soon her hope turns into despair and she becomes "earth" the ultimate station of all pain inflicted to. Her agony pertaining to child-birth goes intensified with the lose of physical charm which cause hsubandial negligence. A kind of mental churning goes endlessly inside Kamala Das as she has a lot of questions relating her body, son, husband, family and society. "............the man who brands you / with his lust but is /shed a slough at end of each embrace."

The "lightning and rain" outwardly manifests "the soft stir in the womb", the both activities bring out "toadstool" that does not signify the mother's agony. The outcome of mother's general and labour pain do not underline her sacrifice for society and family. The mother instinct in a woman is the central cause of her subjection argues "Nancy Chorodow in her book *The Reproduction of Mothering* (1978) sets out to explore why women choose to mother. She rejects the idea that mothering is an innate and natural instinct and equally the idea it is merely the result of social conditioning ...."[27]

The contention if motherhood is natural or conditioned by social customs get poetically rectified in the following lines,:

> When the rain ceased
> And the light was gay on our casuarinas leaves
> Wailing into the light he came
> So fair, a streak of light thrust
> Into a fading light. They raised him
> To me then
> Proud Jaisurya.

Coming and fading of light promptly suggest the mood of mother of Kamala Das. She is tossed in twilight of happiness and melancholy. Again she recalls the darkness that was in the womb and the darkness that surrounds her mind because of newly born babe's responsibility. She is placed in a dilemma of unspeakable nature with the birth of son Jaisurya. Certain celebrations in the life of women become the cause of de-celebration, such an event is birth of a child as a consequence of "Mortal Love". The poem "Mortal Love" focuses on high sounding words like "fidelity" and chastity which according to author do not suit worldly love affairs which is absolutely calculative and business like matter. Terms and conditions applied in heaven in love cannot apply in worldly love affairs. The final verdict of Kamala Das in this matter is, "For you / and me life is too short / for absolute bliss and much too long alas for constancy." The nature of our world is temporary so is the nature of love over here, on the other hand love in "other world" is eternal blissful constant and tinged with heavenly fidelity comments Kamala Das.

The foregoing analytical and thematic study of these poems reveals that author's war against rotten patriarchy is continuing and she is conscious of feminist attitude to beauty. The concept of feminist aesthetics indoctrinated by male mind is not acceptable as it bears no opinion of women at large. It contains poisonous seed of subjection and subordination of women in every matter of family and society. The author understands very well the ancient strategy of men's against women in the garb of honeyed words of religion, aesthetics and domesticity. As far as Hindu mythology is concerned she borrows the unique myth of Radha-Krishna as an ideal destination of worldly love. Radha-Krishna myth does not involve in the writing of Kamala Das any bit of spirituality or salvation which other writes do. Other components of Radha - Krishna such as Vrindavan, Kadamb and river yamuna intensify Kamala Das's desire to highlight this sort of love. The contemporary issues pertaining husband - wife relationship have found adequate attention in many poems. The debate of "nudity" in contemporary society gets wider platform which according to Kamala Das is need of the time to show corporal strength a woman has been gifted with by nature in order to enslave male psyche. In the discourse of Sigmund Freud male strength is shown by genital part and that women has been deprived of any such organ hence held weak. She goes on arguing that women's body structures has more natural grace and fascination to attract man if only once they are conscious of it. Frequent use of "prisoner", "fail", "weeds" "freaks" and "convicts" like words show that there is a long gap between male domain and women's war to re-capture it. The war is not easy to reach its target as the social norms and structures are man-oriented in its functioning. However she has not put the weapon aside. She further understands that fragile social systems shows better glamour and anger together to divert the attention of feminist war. These poems are best example of Kamala Das's mood and mission to establish women on the zenith of society fully conscious of their all round beauty and inherent space for humanity at large.

References and works cited

1. N.V. Raveendran, *Aesthetics of Sensuality,* p. 85.
2. Jane Freedman, *Feminism,* (Intro), p. 1.
3. Jane Freedman, *Feminism,* (New Delhi: Viva Book), p. 19.
4. *Ibid,* p. 18.
5. *Ibid,* Pp. 13.14.
6. M.K. Naik, *A History of Indian English Literature,* (New Delhi: Sahitya Academy.), p. 208.
7. R.K. Srinivas Iyengar, *Indian Writing in English* (New Delhi: Sterling Pub.), p. 678.
8. Jane Freedman, *Feminism,* p. 4.
9. R. Mittapalli & Pier Paolo Picincco, *Kamala Das: A Critical Spectrum,* p. 22.
10. *Ibid,* p. 23.
11. A.N. Dwivedi, *Kamala Das and Her Poetry,* p. 69.
12. *Ibid,* p. 66.
13. Meena Alexander, *Women in Romanticism* (New Delhi-orient Longman). p. 3.
14. Linda Hutcheon, *The Politics of Postmodernism* (London: Rontledge.), p. 150.
15. *Ibid,* p. 154.
16. Meena Alexander, *Women in Romanticism* p. 4.
17. Manju Jaidka, *Recent Trends in Woman's Poetry* (May Faces of Desire: K.Das), p. 83.
18. Jane Freedman, *Feminism,* p. 18.
19. A.N. Dwivedi, *Kamala Das and Her Poetry,* p. 79.
20. Kamala Das, *My Story,* p. 23.
21. A.N. Dwivedi, *Kamala Das and Her Poetry,* p. 35.
22. Harry Balmires, *History of Literary Criticism,* (New Delhi: Macmillan,), p. 376.
23. N.V. Raveendran, *Aesthetics of Sensuality,* p. 122.

24. Manju Jaidka, *Recent Trends in Woman's Poetry*, p. 32.
25. *Ibid*, p. 69.
26. S.N. Singh and N.K. Basu, *Women in Ansient India* (New Delhi: Kamala Pub. 2002), Preface, Pp. VIII-IX.
27. Jane Freedman, *Feminism*, p. 21.

4

Freed Prisoner

Under this chapter those poems are studied which are written during eighties (1971-80). These poems celebrate the success of feminist movement and emancipation of women from socio - domestic barriers. In the year 1971 India under the dynamic leadership of Indira Gandhi freed and re - named East - Pakistan as Bangladesh. Entire glob was taken aback on the spectacular achievement of a women prime minister in India. Her glory was celebrated across the national boundary as a global phenomenon. She became role model for grass root women. All women started looking inside their personality where indomitable energy was stored unused. This was the time when may countries were ruled by women as Bhandar Naike in Sri Lanka, Margret Thatcher in England and Indira Gandhi in India had been global brand ambassador of feminist victory.

On the other hand, patriarchy has began to realize their monopoly in political, social and even familial affairs being on the verge of extinction. By way of legislation women started getting their share in governmental and non - governmental organizations. They have substantial intervention in politics, administration and domestic affairs. They are now not that much dependent on male-money as they were in the last decade. Political social and domestic system along with leadership monopoly have undergone drastic changes because of woman have started projecting their strength in these areas.

Kamala Das in her poems written during aforesaid period raised problem which grew because of shifting focus of society and family consequently affecting husband wife relationship. Wife no matter what social and economic status she belongs to, is for certain to be affected by changes taking place. Inflating purse of women increased amount of greed in husband the other way. As Kamala Das understands well the male psyche; they created new tricks and tools to tarnish women's life strategically. They cannot put weapons of exploitation aside so easily because that reality will throw them on the margin of system.

The chapter's first poem is "Inheritance" which focuses on multi-religious social texture of India. All religions adversely affect the life women. The good and universal elements of religion are not put in practice, rather negative tendencies are underlined by "religion - contractors" it be Imams, Pundits are likewise others. Kamala Das has strong opinion that most fatal force used for subjection of women is misinterpreted scriptures. The women are taught not to interrogate religious beliefs and practices. Kamala Das gives a very derogatory remark on religion as our inheritance. "this ancient / virus that we nurtured in the soul." Religion in the hand of contractors is as fatal as virus creating speed of social evils in the world. The great wars fought across the world were induced by some or the other element of religious virus. :

> When at sundown, the muezzins high wail sounded from
> The mosque, the chapel bells announced the angelus, and
> From the temple rose the brahmin's assonant chant...............

Three main sects of religion Islam, Christianity and

Hinduism in their popular form teach only hatred and sense of supremacy over the other. Kamala Das criticizes this society splitting lesson of religion. And as a true humanist she prefers "that it was only our father's lunacy speaking." Karl Marx also said that religion is an opium dose which rational person should avoid taking. What verdict religion passes for poor men in society is madness and fanaticism. "Slay them who do not / Believe, or better still, disembowel their young ones / and scatter on the street the meager innards." The real picture and intention of religion can be seen in the from of slaying innocent people of other sect. If God has any connection with any religion then religion should be pacific, all embracing, tolerant, loving and caring. How elements of envy, hatred, bloodshed and massacre can enter the genuine spirit of religiosity? The binding line is a prayer creating distinction between misread text of religion and God. She utters,

> Oh God,
> Blessed be your fair name
> Blessed be the religion
> Purified in the unbeliever's blood blessed be
> Our sacred city, blessed be its incarnadined glory.

The poem "Inheritance" is a testimony of author's concern for more serious and universal issues hovering around the globe. Mina-Surjeet Singh optly remarks that "She (Kamala Das) hopes that here will be a day when religious beliefs would not be held against anyone but will be a tribute to the persons moral strength."[1] Those who believe Kamala Das to be a poet of feminist orientation should re - consider that she is humanist endowed with wider-global consciousness.

The idea conveyed in the poem "The Cart Horse" is all about how after a stage author's word power go decrepit and impotent in expressing deep human concerns of the author. Experience and their verbal communication stands apart in substance. Kamala Das has been suffering social and domestic stigma since the date she realized her individuality which cannot be linguistically externalized. She wants to give rest to her mind, body and language as they all have gone "poor thing". The path they have being treading is too "arduous / And its burden always / Too heavy." The horse (words) who die on road is lucky because those who come and go through the road can understand what amount of pain the horse passed through. The image of a dying horse resembles the physical conditions of Kamala Das and her dictional impotency.

> And old horse,
> If lucky, dies on road
> Flopping on its side with
> Pink foam spurting form its
> Twisted jaw and four of
> Yellow front teeth showing.

Kamala Das like a old horse has been fighting by pen and person for the feminist cause is tired and exhausted but zeal inside is yet not extinguished. There are another troop of horses like her battling for the same cause. But the factor of fortune contributes a lot in elevating the horse form ordinary to extraordinary condition. "The not so lucky are / Taken out and shot................." Out of these two conditions Kamala Das endorses the previous one because death for a noble cause is better than being shot dead. In between two there exists one parasite sucking blood and wealth of battling and those who are rowed to be shot dead.

> ....the rich who sit with
> There keeper on benches
> Beside the sea wall, with
> Cataract on their minds
> Tremble at this sound, for
> No reason the old ones
> Purse their mouths and tremble.

The society of women with tradition burdened walk and

myopic vision despite seeing and knowing the hellish condition of theirs keep mum and inert. They are the real culprit because of mental and physical inertia against ancient exploitation. In a way Kamala Das warns battling group of women to keep away from such greedy selfish and cataracted society, who is good for noting. The social and intellectual battle do not go weak because of enemy but because of fake and fraud supporters. The winning stage of women has secured a respectable place for them in postmodern scenario contends Linda Hutcheon.:

> Few would disagree today that feminism have transformed art practice: through new forms, new self consciousness about representation and new awareness of both contexts and particularities of gendered experience. They have certainly make women artists more aware of themselves as women as artist, they are even changing men's sense of themselves as gendered artists.[2]

Identification of woman as woman and as a gendered artist came about by the way Kamala Das argues that by battling not only against evident odds but inherent dissonance elements too. Removal of confusion about the role of women is must for lucid existence and esteemed recognition.

The life of women in society most often goes through pangs of humiliation maintains Kamala Das. In a way entire social system is like a trauma centre where women are tethered but once Kamala Das also happened to get admitted to "The Intensive Cardiac Care Unit" a place lesser painful and a bit freer from social sneer. She views this care unit as worthier than society. "The intensive cardiac care unit / is where the weary traveller pauses to pitch a tent, the oasis / for a night's rest before the long crossing / on camelback." What makes intensive care unit an oasis and an appropriate place to pitch a tent for a night is that no relatives and known connection are allowed to intervene the artificial and mecharized rest period of patient. The rest of society and kindred's are depicted as a vast desert which Kamala Das is tired of crossing on the camelback. The endless fatigue in crossing the desert of relationships is intolerable in comparison to physical pain which one undergoes in cardiac care unit. Again the poet says "the intensive cardiac care unit is where each lies in his own while tent / under harsh desert moons / buried only neck deep in sleep..........." The patient Kamala Das awaits for execution of operation on her body. But what will be the immediate and ultimate effect of operation haunts like a nightmare around the patient's bed. In such a condition "moody as distant drums sound the heartbeat." Another vision of "intensive cardiac care unit / is where the tall dark doctor comes at might night visiting / called up from the depths of dreams out of breath................" The doctors also present a horrible picture but not that much which society presents for Kamala Das. And amid these nasty surrounding the author has to compare her outside condition with that of inside intensive care unit. She finally compares her with "a vagrant cow nods its head and moves on". Neither here in care unit nor elsewhere she finds satisfaction of body and mind so keeps her search on to a place she has to construct by her own feminist tools and principles. "There is no doubt Kamala Das is a new phenomenon in Indo-Anglian poetry-a far cry indeed from Toru Datt or even Sarojini Naidu. Kamala Das is a fiercely feminine sensibility that dares without inhibitions to articulate the hurts she has received in an insensitive largely man - made world,"[3] comments R.K. Srinivas Iyenger. Kamala Das along with her poetic talent is a avowed sympathizer with women's common pangs. She always attempts to create new methodology and life - style for women that is always against man - made patterns of society. Incessant struggle of Kamala Das with phallocentric mentality has made her habitual to shocks and blows of death resembling pains. "The floods of death / have receded ....all I remember is life's growing pain" is the substance of the poem "Ethics" under scanner, and also the foundation of aesthetics Kamala Das wants to construct for new age women. Death is not that much painful as the continuing "pain" that revives women from mental numbness and physical inertia. The striking feature of "Ethics" is divisiveness of the author's self into numerous bits. She denies belonging to these selves initially but all selves united together stand for Kamala Das. "If someone were to ask me now, who / was that sick woman in room number 565, / I would feel tempted to say, not I."

Physical and mental sickness of various varieties have struck many times the body of Kamala Das so much so that she has forgotten name of the diseases and hospitals and other details. Whatever has been the condition of Kamala Das her kith and kins have stereotyped response every time "This night / he smiles at me, on my verandah / under a rash of winter - stars, he smiles." The "smile" of some so-called dear and near is ironical and paining to Kamala Das. Her view exposes the true nature of relationship, "the busy man must always smile at love." Whatever be the condition of wife a busy man (Kamala Das's husband) must keep smiling to reveal his over tight schedule of work. The scene that follows next truly exhibits fake and lusty temperament of wedlock. :

> Idly they caress
> my brow, my lips, my breast, ethically
> he cannot afford more. My eyes fill
> with tears. So might - poor Eve have wept
> tempting in vain not her man
> but her handsome creator...........

Adam the creator of Eve is the central cause of her tearful eyes so is the man of today is the main cause of women's crying. Kamala Das understands well that focus of man is carnal utility of woman except that she is destined to suffer physical and mental agony. M.K. Naik has made a laudable study of Kamala Das's poetic themes, "she may 'flaunt .... A grand flamboyant lust' but in heart of hearts she remains the eternal Eve proudly celebrating the essential feminity."[4]

In an age of post modernity where established social and ethical values are basically trashed, Kamala Das has deep sense of reverence for Radha - Krishna myth and tearful eyes of Eve. This attitude of Kamala Das justifies that in breaking new path she does not hesitate taking aid from any ancient and mythological resource. Her pathway to contemporary aesthetics is both innovative and conservative upto a reasonable extent. The complete work of Kamala Das laments the lose of grand - mother who by and large supported the author for feminist compassion and fresher approach towards humanity. In the present poem "The Millionaires at Marine Drive" she remembers her grandmother's absence as "an ache still persists." After compassionate grandmother's death Kamala Das has to encounter numerous afflictions all alone. Physical properties of grandmother have been buried under soil after last ceremony but it is "soil of my heart" that she is still present with all her totality. All day and night Kamala Das recalls that grandmother with her death has taken away every thing Kamala Das loved and lived with. The mental agony the poet felt after grandmother's final departure is heart breaking. :

> No longer was
> There someone to put an arm around my
> Shoulders without a purpose, all the hands,
> The great brown thieving hands groped beneath my
> Cloths, their fire was that of an arsonist's,
> Warmth was not their aim, they burt my cities
> Down.

Grandmother's loving hold of author's shoulder and "other" holds are pole apart. Grandmother's touch is encouraging, loving and compassionate and husband's touch as a busy man is for extortion and greed. The difference Kamala Das notices between motherhood and worldliness. The burning of Kamala Das's city is metaphor for anger and irritation enticed by the carnal touch of husband devoid of genuine love and co - feeling. The rendering of author's inner feeling into poetic diction is more close to physical experience.:

> ....it was not blood but acid that flowed
> Through my arteries and in autumn years
> I yellowed, sickened like leaves on trees
> Gained a freedom I never once had asked for.

The grandmotherly touch gives life, energy, enthusiasm and cause to live for Kamala Das and other's selfish love snatches above things away from and makes her sick for ever. The millionaire of Marine Drive scatters grains (things to tempt Kamala Das) to his lusty web. Once in the green and loving shade of grandmother's love she was flittering in glee but after marriage she is a beautiful "dove" tempted by lusty millionaire husband to his acid-clutch of sexuality. Only stage and characters do change but the plot of drama remains unchanged as far as the life of women is concerned states author in the final section of the poem. "The party goes, the guests only / change their painted masks but I see nothing / But the fog of their hate ....but / surely ....lovers still cling with wet / Limbs, we eyes near doorways at parting hour?

The destiny of women face one hand compassionate touch of grandmother's, on the other selfish, greedy and sexual embrace of husband's and lover's which both narrate the true situation of women in the world. The thesis derived from the discourse is appropriately summed up in the following statement, :

> But sexist ideology, necessarily promotes the concept of 'woman - as - object or woman - as - other; Josphine Denovan insists that this is a moral, not just an aesthetic issue, she formulates the stereotypes of women in western literature good and evil, virgin, ideal and sex object, inspirer or seductress as vehicle of salvation or destruction for the male heroes. [5]

The male attitude classifying women into different categories does not justify their social and domestic roles. The male categorization blur the path of women as they are stereotyped on the guidelines of man is the theme of "The

Blind Walk". Women walk in life almost blind, deaf and lame. They are deprived of even their own body, mind and vision which are colonized by male sovereignty. The entire portrayal is made in symbolic manner, "mango trees are turning brown", the cold poisonous breath of the sea follows me", "feeble rain throbs on the city's brow like migraine" are indicative of desperation of women in the society mainly dominated by men. The author has left back her "glasses" so her walk today is to be "blind walk", the blind walk is symbolic of life's walk in the real sense. Women's mechanical life sans individual choice and vision is without enthusiasm and individual purposefulness. Like a puppet they operate on the command of men laments Kamala Das that is ghost like shadowy experience. Her tiredness and nausea is reflected in the following images, "red buses", "felled lover's tree" and "the dark" are suggestive of destructive elements which Kamala Das wants to tempt to crush as she is lost of energy to walk any longer blind eyed. Her search of "eye" that can show beautiful and ugly, friend and enemy and trench and mount is essential for creation of wholesome feminist personality. Borrowed or imposed vision is worse than no vision at all maintains the author. The whereabouts of Kamala Das's city in these days is unknown and settled by strangers so she has lost her ways many times. The strangeness of city the author feels because of altered attitude of society, :

> he was the only landmark I could
> recognize his name is the only name I
> remember sweet and unuttered it lies
> cradled in my breath the poet's ultimately
> lose their way inside their own minds

The poem "The Blind walk" is all about lose of women's identity in the zig-zag ways of domesticity. The poet revisits her past to find only "Caracasses" in the river of memory. The opinion of the author forwarded in this poem is that not only present is polluted and blinded of women but romantic future and past are also badly spoiled by male mindset. The only way for them is to find "vision" and "plan" of their own by fight otherwise they have to meet deeper subjection. This is the process of creation of fresh life style and aesthetic sensibility. The poem "The Blind Walk" is clarion call for all voiceless and visionless women to recollect their strength of mind and body. A.N. Dwivedi's study of woman persona in Kamala Das 's writing is apt enough to the occasion, "the woman - persona in her asserts an 'indomitable will' and the 'spirit of revenge' (to use Millon's popular phrase) and gives a clarion - call to the weaker sex to rise in revolt against all kinds of repression and tyranny being perpetrated on it."[6]

The "spirit of revenge" added with desire to make a new territory of their own Kamala Das presses these ideas in "The Proud One". "Young man's most normal desire is to subjugate a girl" it is a sort of victory over nature gifted territory of women - that is her body. The mal intention of man is to use that body like a toy and then spurn it to dust. Reaction to this attitude is very stunning when Kamala Das revolts like, "the old wife turned whorish and withdrew from under him?" One must not confuse that Kamala Das promotes whorism in matrimonial relation rather she presents resentment over derogatory treatment wives very often receive from the side of husbands. Such a rotten and selfish relationship she does not like to continue so comments thus, "...............but loving him, / I found no courage then even to be kind." She has shunned even showing kindness and love to such husband Now on she has to move herself alone keeping eyes open and vision clear for future plans of feminism.

Since the man - woman relation has reached the peak of emotional stagnation which Kamala Das utters in "Autumn Leaves" a very small poem containing the seed of separation. "I saw his chest / and all that hair / and, on that very night in my dream / autumn winds blew ....," falling of leaves from the trees and new shoots coming upon the branches. To use the Shelleyan phrase "If winter comes can spring be far behind?" The answer of Kamala Das is in positive note like Shelley because she is sure of success in the liberation movement of women form the confinement of centuries old patriarchy. Kamala Das finds all sorts of satisfaction in presenting male and female body as an active participant of ancient war. She says:

> ....women should derive satisfaction out of their sexuality, challenging sexual norms. This could be through watching nude male body (his chest and all that hair) standing nude with him (Looking Glass) and enjoying all that the male body offers for pleasures. Hence Kamala Das's speaker seems to mean that woman should endeavour to know herself through sexual union.[7]

In the writing of Kamala Das main focus goes on knowing womenfolk no matter it happens by way of copulation or nudity or other erotic means. In the endeavour of knowing feminist identity she composes and de - composes her body and mind several times is the theme of a long poem titled "Composition". The proper composition consists of body, mind, personality, identity and existence that can be known either by systematically de-composing or use the Derridean phrase de-constructing the totality. In this process of revealing oneself (by de-composing or de-constructing) better and deeper understanding develops. Kamala Das plunges into herself and comes out with "face to face with the sea". The "sea" is a metaphor for soul the ultimate source of existence and personality. The type of assertive and objective poetry Kamala Das has been writing so far presents a contrast here, "This is the contradiction between the form of her utterance and its topic and content. This is what creates the ambivalence necessitates self-reflection and realizing the inappropriateness of indirect assertion breaks the linguistic double bind"[8], comments N.V. Ravindran. The "sea" metaphor offers physical and mental interplay which goes on ever is the search of speaker's identity. As readers of Kamala Das are familiar with grandmother's love has vital and sea share in the making of author's revolting personality. She admits, "Lying beside my grandmother, quite often I thought / that I could hear at night / the surf breaking on the shore." Grandmother's memory is a fountain of energy and cause of author's personality enlargement. Author is unaware of internal sea and its inherent energy she has been learning "lesson of self-betrayal". Getting betrayed by relations is not that much dangerous as by own self, feels the author at this stage of self-inspection. "The red house" where author was born and reared in the loving and passionate touch of grandmother is crumbling and the old grandmother has died of paralysis. Her body was deformed by old age that she was incapable of walking for daily scores. Kamala Das has a mixed response to her parental house and grandmother's loving attitude, "love and hate are / involvements. But this only signifies growth / and, growth is natural. The tragedy of life is not death but growth. Death is rather end of tragedy and growth a big start into the sorrowful territory of tragedy. As women grow by body and mind their tragic life begins Kamala Das states. From the soothing lap of grandmother to young age her growth signifies stepping into matrimonial gradual death. She has no time for outer and inner "sea" that occasionally visited her dreams. The image of "sea" stands for freedom, energy and vastness which Kamala Das lacks since the date she became bride.

> When I got married
> My husband said
> You may have freedom
> As much as you want.
> My soul balked at this diet of ash.
> Freedom became my dancing shoe
> How well I danced,
> And danced without rest,

The freedom granted by husband for Kamala Das is a joke which can only eradicate individual identity and subjugate her. She asked her husband in the tone of suspicion, 'am I hetero / am I lesbian / or am just plain frigid?" these question have no answer but self - inspection which author does every now and then whenever here comes the issue of contemporary feminist freedom. Kamala Das in matter of sexuality celebrates her freedom from every possible angle in order to counter male sexuality. :

> I have lost my best friend
> to a middle - aged queer
> The lesbians hiss their love at me.
> love
> I no longer need,
> with tenderness I most content,
> I have learnt that friendship
> cannot endure...............

Sexuality and love are two distinct things which cannot be taken to be one and identical says Kamala Das. Her husband only needed her body as a stage of sexual play. She finds herself "so alone" and "missed her grandmother". Her grandmother always took care of Kamala Das and helped avoiding the pangs of loneliness. Any reader can maintain the author to be "a girl with vast / sexual hungers / a bitch after my (his) heart." This is not the truth of Kamala Das's married life, she wants love and mutual understanding more than carnal satisfaction. The reversal of situation (first - sexuality and no love) is a brutal and barbaric behaviour which she never admits. Her reaction and hatred towards male approach to sexuality is expressed like this, "Grovel at my feet / remove your monkey suits and dance / sing Erato, Erato, Erato / Yet I shall be indifferent." Her indifference towards patriarchal view of sexuality is a question of sexual ambivalence which she wants to construct for current and succeeding generations. Women of every clime and creed have same problem in affairs of love and sexuality.

> We are all alike
> We women
> in our wrappings of hairless skin,

All skeletons are alike
Only the soul's vary
that hide somewhere between the flesh
and the bone,
skin a human being and he will
still breathe..........

The personality of woman is bifurcated into "physicality" and "individuality" by the author, the proper combination of the two constitutes proper personality fit for love and sexuality. This issue was raised by D.H. Lawrence in his *Sons and Lovers* by different character personifying flesh and intellect separately. The quality of soul and spirit is not inborn, rather it needs inculcation and regular practice by individuals which husband of Kamala Das basically lacks. The popular opinion held of feminist identity is that they are in the struggling process of realization in India and abroad. :

Recent critics and historians have argued that the feminist battle for individual rights was considerably more successful in colonies than at home. "While European civil society remained undecided as to whether women possessed the attributes and capacities of individuals, its colonial counterparts - in places like India was more amenable to the good offices of the white female subject.[9]

Kamala Das does not support the view that European society being economically stronger is ahead in matters of feminist welfare. She values more the attributes of mind and behavior than that of body and wealth. Every women stripped "of skin and flesh" has power to enthrall male mind for sexual desire but the basic structure "skeleton is dead / and most different to soul". The reference to "soul" does not invite metaphysical interpretation rather it explains behaviour, self - rcspect, sense of co - existence and over all individual freedom. The author turns back into "flashback" where grandmother a fountain of eternal love, ideal womanhood and energy Kamala Das finds in abundance. Her grandmother "kept a lighted lantern / on the window-sill". The image of "lighted lantern / on window-sill is indicative of past and present memory by mental configuration way of grandmother and Kamala Das. The house once owned by grandmother had been flooded with love and compassion is now decaying in terms of structure and love symbolically shown by "its rafters shook in the wind." Kamala Das kept engrossed in talk with Grandmother whole night. "My grandmother's lamp burnt all night." Her intimate conversation was full of soul and energy that author expresses, "by peeling off my layers / I reach closer to the soul". This ordinary events of Kamala Das's life may sound ordinary but the massage contained is universally important for feminist point of view. The first school Kamala Das joined for education never provided women-friendly knowledge therefore she utters in disgust, "My first School-house / is now a brothel". The education provided by typical school is defunct and beautification of women's body comes to an end "for the roaring night." Apart form corporal beauty women are deprived of self-respect and identity such is the impact of education. Their life is no longer their own but a lavish preparation for husband to "devour". The author's advice to women community is:

> Here is my advice to you.
> Obey each other's crazy commands
> Ignore the sane.
> Turn you home into a merry
> Dog - house
> Marriage is meant to be all this...........
> ....anyway most humorous heaven.

Kamala Das has realized the futility of conventional marriage-bonds, love-oaths and mutual assurances. She now wants to forgive all those who have cheated betrayed and went infidel in love. The state of total "forgiveness" in Kamala Das is indicative of her diversion from rotten social conventions to new aesthetics building on doctrine of humanism. She has finally realized her "uselessness" in the mess of patriarchal system therefore opts to move "to take a long walk / into sea / and lie there, resting, /completely uninvolved." In the life of women and men there are numerous "childish whim", "minor hunger" and "larger hunger" but "at the basement of the sea" there lurks hungers of dignity and existence which take a long time of battle to realize. "The potent fragments of oneself" according to Kamala Das is different basic selves of personality unity of which is prerequisite of individuality and meaningful projection of the same. Her proposition of feminist identity is given below:

> The ultimate discovery will be
> that we are immortal,
> the only things mortal being
> even our pains continuing
> in the devourers who constitute
> the world.
> ....
> my only freedom being
> the freedom to discompose.

In the process of decomposition lie hidden the elements of feminist freedom. And immortality which Kamala Das focused in this poem is a search of "sea" and self the eternal source of energy, freedom and beauty by virtue of which she can avoid her fragmentation of personality. "...........her poems explore not only the self but also the universal experience of women. These explorations go beyond the limitations of feminism. While exploring the problems of the women her poems embrace the problem of humanity in general."[10] Any scholarly who claim that Kamala Das is only a poet of feminist longings is parochial and unfit to make balanced appraisal. My attempt to locate Kamala Das as a maker of fresh feminist aesthetics finds validity and impetus from many such poems.

The popular concept of aesthetics does not match with that of Kamala Das as the poem "Sunset, Blue bird" too hints towards. Kamala Das like an ideal and faithful wife keeps her mind always attached to husband's memory whereas he behaves in a wanton way. People "warned not to go near the king" (husband). She wants equal and humanistic attitude but "he clutched me to his breast, he said he loved me." The "love" has different meaning for author and her husband; all polar different. The kind of sexual love husband makes "after a year two moon waxed and waned without a sing of blood." The personality of author as a woman is not cared for, not her consent is sought for erotic pleasure. After the monotony of sexuality the life becomes dark without sun. The sunset has stepped in Kamala Das's life forever where no dawn is possible only "blue bird" keeps flying in the sky of her imaginative mind. Many phrases are repeated in "Sunset, Blue bird" as a poetic device to intensity the apart hood existent between husband and wife, and body and mind. "Repetition is the fundamental constitutive principle of free - verse (prose - poetry). In free - verse forms and inter relations are represented by verbal or thematic reiteration."[11]

Kamala Das reiterates her denial of conventionality and admits validity of positive and humanistic individualism in "A New City" which she visited ignoring her previous belongings and relationships. The futility of wedlock is hinted at by "a picnic bag" with which she joined the relation "to seek a blind date". The absolute value of sex oriented marriage life is "to shed as snakes do in coils and coils / my weariness." Her plan for future is to build a new city where love, cooperation, understanding dwell between males and females. With utmost honesty she utters of new city's blue print.

> I have come, yes, with hunger, with faith and a secret language
> all ready to be used. I have come with a picnic bag
> to this new city to seek a blind date.

The poems written after the publication of *The Old Playhouse and Other Poems* are wide and deep in humanistic concerns. "..................there is little amount of erotica. Rather they deal with other deeply personal and universal themes.

One might, therefore, feel that erotica has been a phase in poet's life,"[12] opines N.V. Raveendran - Erotica has never been destination of Kamala Das's writing rather an important side of husband-wife relationship. Whenever sound relationship of man-woman goes imbalanced there is single reason that is demand of "erotica" from male partner denying other nice aspects of female's personality. This selfish attitude creates mental and physical illness well depicted in "Cerebral Thrombosis". It is a serious mental illness which implies other personality disorders as an inevitable consequence. A relation of the author has been under medical care for treatment of cerebral thrombosis, the picture of that patient applies to average man and woman of our society. The throat of the patient produces a sound similar to "oxcart wheels on gravel", and previously was "fluted hear" but now there is "ballads of sea". How this drastic change came about is a concern of all of us. It is both medical and behavioral challenge for modern society that we have disowned our elderly persons on their own luck. :

> He was past eighty
> Yet it was an adolescent
> Dream that prowled the dirt-road of his brain.

Kamala Das has been victim of male mentality along with her mother, however her compassionate heart wants to take personal care of elderly people suffering from cerebral thrombosis despite his "dirty - road of his brain". His relatives are "sleep - obsessed", "weary" and eagerly waiting for his final departure to feel free of familial formalities. On the other hand Kamala Das genuinely shows sympathy of mind and hand by coming forward to share the pain. I can assert in her poetic territory there lives love and compassion for all suffering males and females above sexuality and erotic manifestation.

The problems faced by humanity across the world are concern of Kamala Das, not only of women of India. The contours of her personality that she has developed and that of Malabar (the place where she was born) have good share in the themes and contents of her poetry, "that can be found in "The Swamp". The swamp has taken root in the mind of Kamala Das, because of stagnation, rigidity and staleness. "My feet cracked the grey crust and I sank with a wail". The lover of Kamala Das complains of his condition not appreciated by beloved. "This tragic spot that has made of us its addicts." Both lover and beloved have grown used to despondent life as an unavoidable part of theirs.

After delivery of a child her agony enhances and she was hospitalized in the room no 565 which occurs in many poems as a meaningful number that indicates important shift in the life of author. Her mental and physical convulsion convey her melancholy response to husband. He comes to meet his physical hunger but after confronting all embracing motherly personality of the author feels ashamed. "I call him my baby I hold him to my breast." Two opposite attitudes confront paving way for higher one to prevail, Despite sacrifice and devotion Kamala Das does not find rightful place in the life of husband. She laments her lot, :

> I am the tainted bush the poisonous
> Snakes retreat .... I have no name
> Of my own my past is a desolate
> Terrain where memory life tall
> Trees grow ....

On the other hand she has to make compromise for smooth functioning of married life is:

> He is the richest the strongest the
> Deadliest I lit one thousand and
> One lamps at our snake shrine
> Praying for a mate ....
> He said power and money do not
> Make four but twenty two.........

Kamala Das being elegant and logical in her observation

is at bay from her counterpart whom she calls "like Frankenstein's brutal toy I shall arise one day I shall walk out of his bed one day." The day of separation has arrived in Kamala Das's writing where she has started a fresh journey of self-celebration life Walt Whitman who sings of / myself as an eve of festivity. In this journey of self-celebration there is room for winter and frigidity. Rather lifeless season of snowy winter went of, "new rain and tender shoots of plants" is the theme of "Winter" a poem pregnant with larger meaning of future feminist draft. The surface of feminist earth is covered with new germinations of flowers and vegetation whereas the roots of feminism are going deep into fertility. In the concept of society Kamala Das does not exclude male participation because of their anti feminist attitude. She has an idea of transformation of personality. She says "I loved her body without shame / on winter evenings as cold winds / Chuckled against the window panes." "Several faces of Eve are exhibited here, - woman as sweetheart, flirt, wife woman of the world, mother, middle - aged matron and above all woman as untiring seeker of the nature of the psychological process behind both feminity and masculinity."[13]

In both cases of feminity and masculinity there lies hidden an element of humanity, which in view of the author is more precious and retainable in personality of both. The traits of humanity and compassion must originate and grow for proper structuring of society as is effectively communicated in "The Ancient Mango Tree". The "ancient mango tree" hints at positive part of author's life which is being trampled under feet by barbaric present. In an engaging pen portrayal Kamala Das presents, "a mother's belly / they plucked out with a scalpel". Mother's belly (womb) bears sons and daughter who later mutilate the same organ of reproduction. The secret of motherhood cannot be revealed no matter conjurer be "Alibaba". The "mango tree" stands for love, nostalgia and energy of past, as the author utters,:

> But why did they cut
> down the ancient mango tree where I
> had hung damp nets of dreams to dry?

All dreams Kamala Das has had in early days of childhood are on the verge of getting dried. Another symbol of "boat" Kamala Das on board cannot go for fishing, as her present and past are waterless (lifeless) and so is future. The theme of "death" haunts the memory of the poet in every fragment of time. Manju Jaidka writes of universal feminism in the following words, "nature is female and her world is violated by male insensitivity where Stevie Smith turns to nature or to the creatures of nature, she is in a way snagging the patriarchal world stating her preference for a life devoid of any human attachment (especially male) encroachment."[14] Mother - nature and mother both are encroached upon and tormented mercilessly by insensate and selfish male mentality. Greed and malice turn good soul into darkness of ignorance is the theme of "Bats" metaphor of blindness and mindlessness. Kamala Das's soul is "like a bat that finds itself / in an alien zone of light." So far she has been clouded by dense darkness and "light" is an alien experience. "Deep / into my bones beyond the gaudy / arrogance of blood, pain dips in with / cold finger tips for the last of human prides." Insensate and gaudy atmosphere of which the author has been inseparable part is now faced with alien zone of light, that is also initiation into new definition of feminist aesthetics.

> From stranger to guest, from guest to
> Lover, my beloved, when you take,
> When you at last win, ignore the stain
> Beneath dead eyes, the fatigue in my smile.

"Dead eyes" and "fatigue in smile" adequately denote the past of the poet but still painful memories of womanhood has been haunting Kamala Das for many years. But at present "Bat" has initialed into new zone of enlightment of mind. Like Emile Dickinson's assertion "Much Madness is the divinest sense." Kamala Das also utters "nothing holds like pain" is the basic mantra of "Ischemia in August." She compares her body as carcass through which blood has stopped circulating. Circulating blood gives life to author whereas pain tenders a peg to hand same life with. True and visible attributes of women's life is pain and circulation of blood through almost lifeless body.

Kamala Das hopefully waits for "Tomorrow" as harbinger of happiness but meets with "chain stronger" to tie her with rotten conventions of patriarchy. Though being a woman she is already chained in feminist "Cowardice" which is expected to go up because they (kith and kins) plan to "rape me with bayonet and hang me for my doubts." Typical characteristics of woman are "cowardice", and "doubt" about ownself that makes their life more miserable. By rusted and worn out weapon women cannot improve their life oppressed and tarnished from every side by patriarchy. "Courage is the blood's silent flowing out of wounds," for Kamala Das because wound denotes fight that approves courage and desire to live life on terms of her own. This kind of attitude can shape "Tomorrow" otherwise future is dark for certain. Fear of death is like huming bird that will come when will come. Kamala Das like Shakespeare asserts "Cowards" die many times before death, valiant tastes death but once". The story of life of tomorrow without courage blood, and wound cannot be made meaningful. The life remains "a story half told" that unfolds the truth of women's life. She goes on painting the inherent structure of women, :

> Resident Gods
> Seal the high notes of pain, still faltering will's
> Ultimate groan, grant
> Me silence below the gallows.........

The turmoil of Kamala Das's life has many twist and turn. There are pain, wail, groan and gallows that prepare conventional foundation of feminism which Kamala Das wants to substitute by hope, victory and self-satisfaction as the basic structure of tomorrow's feminist aesthetics of women which the author repeats in the concluding part:

> Tomorrow they may bind me with chains stronger that
> Those of my cowardice, rape me with bayonets and
> Hang me for my doubts.........

Hope and despair rotates in the life of Kamala Das like light and drk yet she has sure commitment to better her tomorrow by even shedding blood. The show of good and evil in the life of battling women (like Kamala Das) is comparable with Margaret Atwood, who "is concerned about these unpleasant aspects of human life. Deeply committed to the cause of women Atwood focuses on how women have a raw deal at the hands of men, how their defenses are undermined in various ways ....how they are subjected to violence, physical, psychological and sexual."[15] The flood of various violence engineered by male hand rendered feminist life as a dark hell which Kamala Das wants to alter and improve at any cost.

The period of "The Stone Age" is about to finish because women have decided to launch a final war of existence in twenty first century. They have been allotted alluring attributes which Kamala Das as a pioneer wants to rectify by her piercing judgment. She states remorsefully, "you turn me into a bird of stone a granite dove." A bird of granite can be lovable but definitely incapable of flight. The lack of free flight is subjugated state of feminist life that Kamala Das shows:

> You built round me a shabby drawing foom
> And stroke my face absentmindedly while you read.
> With loud talk
> You bruise my pre-morning sleep
> You stick a finger into my dreaming eye.

"Striking of face" while reading, "bruising pre-morning sleep" and "sticking a finger into dreaming eye" are suggestive of Kamala Das's life getting unnecessary patriarchal intervention. These practices are husbandial conventions taken for granted which women are bound to tolerate. During working hours as housewives or working women they are to be "shadowed down" as a mark of humiliation and inferior condition. The conflict going on in between man and woman for existence can be understood as "secretly flowing drains / beneath sacred cities." The "sacred cities" are women's life and "flowing drains secretly" are ill-treatment given to women at different occasions. Kamala Das alters her ill - treatment with outer and internal freedom that she presents thus, "I drive my blue battered car / along the blue sea". Blue coloure is loved by author as symbol of vast freedom which she finds inside her personality. In the process of intro-extro inspection Kamala Das happens to visit neighbours, friends and foes, who "watch me (poet) come and go like rain". She concludes that men are assumed lion because women are feeble goats. The lion has inborn instinct to kill the goats (women) or set them free on their mercy. The total personality of women is second rate and imposed which author does not like to endorse.

> ask me the flavour of his mouth, ask me
> why his hand sways like a hooded snake
> before it clasps my publis. Ask me why
> like a great tree, felled, he stumps against my breasts
> and sleeps. Ask me why life is short
> and love is shorter still, akd me what
> is bliss and what its price.................

A woman like Kamala Das has abundant knowledge of husband's life (a hooded snake) but her knowledge about herself is very sleek by dint of which identity cannot be built and projected. Stevie Smith in the fashion of Kamala Das very softly but steadily opposes different institutions of authoritism. "Stevie Smith is also Blakean in her rejection of authority. She seems to agree with William Blake that the church, the parent and the teacher are all evil institutions bent on distorting one's personality, crushing the individual growth of a person."[16] The main target of attack in Kamala

Das's writing isnot an individual but the spirit of subjection no matter it dwells in behaviour of male or female. Her feminist courtyard is wide enough to admit whoever comes with fair intention of humanity and justice for all.

Man's devouring attitude she not only dislikes but wants to crash strategically is well stated in "The Lion in Siesta". The adjective "lion" is attached to man's violent behaviour towards women." His claws are / neatly manicured, his long mane smells / of the flowers she wears." To satisfy his eroticism the man wants women's intimacy afterwards leave her to nothingness. The parental house owned and enlivened by grand mother's presence and compassion has vital role in the life of Kamala Das as a poet. "The Old Play House" is a central poem in the collection *The Old Play House and other Poems* dealing with the theme and definition of house as the poet wishes to built and sustain in her life. The poem develops with the metaphor of freedom "Swallow" who wants to soar high in sky ignoring "the long summer of your love." The "raw seasons" are fit for birds to face hard wind and gale in comparison to domestic summer season of love. What captivates freedom lovers is "endless pathways of sky." One hand sky is the limit for the bird (wife) on the other there is narrow place of husbandial dominance. Kamala Das's preference goes with freedom which she finds in education, development of personality and building of self-recognition. These main constituents and more are the corner stones of her notion of contemporary women's aesthetics. :

> I was not to gather knowledge
> Of yet another man that I came to you but to learn
> What I was and by learning, to learn to grow but every
> Lesson you gave was about your self.

Knowledge and lesson about husband as a "another man" is not the target to Kamala Das but adverse situations of family and patriarchal challenge. The corporal intimacy any woman usually enjoys with male partner is significant but enlargement of personality is most important for Kamala Das as a path breaking author. She sneers the monotonous application of mind and body:

> You were pleased
> With my body's response, its weather, its usual shallow
> Convulsions you dribbled spittle into my mouth your poured
> Yourself into every nook and cranny, you embalmed
> My poor lust lust with your bitter - sweet juices you called my wife.

Certain words in these lines may indicate the description to be pornographic, such as "body's response, its weather," "shallow convulsion", "you dribbled spittle into my mouth", "you embalmed my poor lust" and "your bitter sweet - juices" however the author's intention is to paint dwarfish condition of women before monstrous ego of men as husband and lover in every affair of family. The definition of wife shown above is not admittable to Kamala Das rather a large number of fresh aspects she wants to include. Taking care of parasite husband is humanistically good but sacrificing total existence and life prospects is mere stupidity maintains Kamala Das. Subjection of absolute feminist personality to monstrous husband is shown by "I ate the magic loaf, I became a dwarf". / I lost my will and reason to all your / questions I mumbled incoherent replies." These sentences indicate volatile existence of women before masculine monarchs.

Kamala Das in order to specify low but battling stance of women creates contrasts which gives better access to ground reality. She offers for new generation feminist authors to use masculine vocabulary as the same was done in Europe during post war literature.

I was only with the coming of post - war novelists such as Irish Murdoch, Muriel Spark, Doris Lessing, Margaret Drabble and Beryl Brain Bridge that we find and authentically female literature representing women's experience and her view of life. They have broken the taboos in their use of vocabulary formerly on all areas of female experience.[17]

Contents of vulgarity may appear to some conventional reader unbearable whereas it works as a rejoinder to male tradition of atrocity, and bold promulgation of new aesthetic dawn. The poem goes with artificial setup of husband's house hated by the author, "your room is always lit by artificial light / windows always shut", "cut flower is vases have began to smell of human sweet" indicate dominating temperament of male mind. In these nauseating climates she feels absence of freshness that is necessary for life, "no more singing, no more dance, my mind is an old playhouse with all its lights put out" convey the reaction of author to the surrounding she is confined by custom. She present an ugly picture of masculinity that "the strong man ....serves his love in lethal doses for love is Narcissus". The flower of Narcissus grows on the bank of husbandial stagnant pond where its fall is inevitable but it also wants space and freedom to live in full. "It must will the mirrors/ to shatter and the kind night to erase the water. "The last line shows paradoxical conditions of women's life wherein "water" is life and mode of Narcissus's drowning.

The idea of sonorous melody as a constituent of aesthetics is contained in "Kumar Gandharva" a poem that beautifully communicates Kamala Das's view of beauty. Beauty of body, mind and personality in always prone to assault, the idea finds poetic expression "cocooned now in song and yet / unsafe". The melody coming out of Kumar Gandharva's song is always at risk to get imbalanced so is the behavioral charm of personality. By way of mild contrast Kamala Das advances her notion of aesthetics :

> ....in every little pause
> My ears must loose their peace and
> Like the silent mouths of fish
> Sucking at the air..............

The urgency of sucking fresh air no one can feel better than the fish out of water so is the value of beauty for women tarnished and humiliated in the hands of men. The concept of beauty differs from male to female paradigm. As far as Kamala Das's stance of aesthetics is concerned it includes with body to brain, personality to identity, dignity to luxury and past to present and future. She has "Glass" in hand to look herself and her all time surrounding to locate her proper identity. The poem "Glass" takes readers to inner journey of women's life which contemporary feminist authors generally avoided in their writings. Kamala Das's visit to her husband for half an hour rendered her as "pure misery, fragile glass, breaking crumbling". She is no longer the same as she was sometimes ago. Her inner structure is broken into mini pieces which cannot be re-shaped because of "monstrous" male centric treatment of husband which Kamala Das offer thus, "its old rafters creaking". The haste of love is not for genuine love but for "hurt and pregnant with pain". She reacts blatantly to this fake love hurry by revealing her agenda of future, "why I did not cry then, broken glass, beware, / why did not tell him that I no longer care whom I hurt with love and often without?"

Feminist surrender to lover is considered by male psyche as a crooked strategy and aversion of love too, Kamala Das defends feminist stand by saying "with a cheap toy's / make of / every trap of lust a temporary home." The fake embrace of husband is sure to meet the same strategic response of wife, because contemporary women have learnt showiness in behaviour. This facial and fake response is the need of hour, "I give a wrapping to their dreams, I give woman - voice, a woman - smell ....and I have misplaced a father some where." The woman has an element of mother and man of father which is largely undermined by deceiving interaction of males. By and large female counterpart retains its innate responsibility as the following argument offers, :

The daughter sense of self and of gender is identified with her mother whereas the sons feel the need to break the attachment to his mother. This differing psychosexual development means that boys grow up with an ability to relate deeply to others but with more of single-minded, competitive values that are necessary for success in public life. Whereas girls grow up to reproduce their mother's capacity to relate to others to nurture and to mother.[18]

The natural distinction of daughters and sons regulate their behaviour as an active members of society. "After the Party" celebrates the natural difference which God has nurtured in males and females for different occasions. From the flow of blood that is evident from body postures, one can easily differentiate the feminist morality from non-feminist. Kamala Das writers, "riven veins unleashing the flood / of that invisible blood." The happiness a woman feels inside her mind is because "of some forgetting". Her memory invariably calls the moments of torture, pain and dejection by the hands of intimate counterparts. When she enters the party she finds "all men dark and sleek like drones / women parakeets offered her chilled hand of severed veins ...." The two extreme creations of nature (man and woman) meet in a party (the world) where the monster man is tempted to devour her. Kamala Das sarcastically says, "........a male glance / And again a smile blazing rudely like alphabets / on kindergartens blackboard tucked neatly away / In memory, the raw letter of lust." The glances of two counterparts have different meaning: the male reads the body of woman as a alphabet of lust, and women reads love, compassion and humanity then lust etc. These apparent differences never let them be one on the platform of marriage or love-affairs mourns Kamala Das. Woman from their part are taught not to make demands but be a thing to be supplied on the demand of male. ".............the fullness of a body, / Tamed by will and practice taught never to make demands." Jane Freedman argues, "Both men's freedom and women's subjection she argues, are created through the original contract with resulting civil freedom being a masculine attribute depending on patriarchal right. Women who are assumed to lack naturally the attributes and capacities of individuals are denied this civil freedom."[19]

In these poems Kamala Das has attepted to break the shackles and re-define horizon of freedom. Broadly she is an author of revolting feminism but a careful and meticulous reader can find underlying seed of harmony and coherence. The positive traits must not be understood as her denial of once taken pledge to uproot unjust patriarchal practices. Her use of Radha - Krishna myth and related references underline the need of harmonious and mutual understating that existed innately between Radha and Krishna as an ideal symbol of marriage-bond. Contemporary elements "three dimensional nudity on weeklies and mouthlies" show that she has no grudge in this kind of feminist manifestation. She argues women should boast of her "physical grace" which God gifted to rule over male lust. There is nothing wrong in winning the battle with the help of "tools" the nature endowed women with. The debate over nudity of women is an uncalled for discourse stirred by greedy male society. All these poems prepare a background of freedom women have been striving to find all their live. And how can the boundaries of confinement can be broken are also poetically suggested here. There is a candid blueprint for future feminism along with expansion of women's sensibility from their domestic to global affairs.

References and works cited

1. Mina Surjeet Singh, *Six Women Poets.* (New Delhi Prestige Publication, 2003), pp. 105-106.
2. Linda Hutcheon, *The Politics of Postmodernism,* p. 139.
3. R.K. Srinivas Iyengar, *Indian Writing in English,* p. 680.
4. M.K. Naik, *A History of Indian English Literature,* (New Delhi: Sahitya Academy.), p. 209.
5. Harry Balmires, *History of Literary Criticism,* (New Delhi: Macmillan,), p. 375.
6. A.N. Dwivedi, *Kamala Das and Her Poetry,* p. 29.
7. N.V. Raveendran, *Aesthetics of Sensuality,* p. 58.
8. *Ibid,* p. 35.

9. Leela Gandhi, *Post Colonial Theory* (New Delhi:OUP), p. 91.
10. N.V. Raveendran, *Aesthetics of Sensuality*, p. 122.
11. *Ibid*, Pp. 134-135.
12. *Ibid*, p. 128.
13. M.K. Naik, *A History of Indian English Literature*, (New Delhi: Sahitya Academy.), p. 209.
14. Manju Jaidka, *Recent Trends in Woman's Poetry*, p. 79.
15. *Ibid*, p. 51.
16. *Ibid*, p. 51.
17. Harry Balmires, *History of Literary Criticism*, (New Delhi: Macmillan,), Pp. 376-377.
18. Jane Freedman, *Feminism*, p. 22.
19. *Ibid*, p. 51.

5

Formation of Aesthetic Territory

The poems studied under this chapter range from 1980 - 90, a period that was last phase of Indira Gandhi's dominance which comes to final closure in 1984 with her assassination. Death of a dominant woman prime minister was a hard blow to feminist movement in India yet her effect on the mind of Indian women was indelible. Every walk of life : politics, education, administration, defence, science and technology have registered women's print. In political parties there have been perennial debate to provide due share of women in legislation. By virtue of spreading education women have proved their inherent potentials. Different feminist organizations have come up over the decade pressing numerous aspects of women's issue. Some undertook education among the under privileged group of society. Some other organization focused on health and poverty eradication. Thus, various aspects of feminist life have been focused, debated and considered for betterment by governmental and volunteer agencies. In a sense this decade may be branded as feminist decade forming its own path and code of conduct.

The waves of deconstruction and liberalization provided global tools for Indian women to re-think and re-construct what has been obsolete ad anti - feminist. They have now international parameter and entire globe as a stage to demonstrate their physical and mental capability. The concept of global citizenship have found momentum and the target Indian women have set to attain is cross cultural and pan-national recognition. In an age of 'post modernity' the idea of local is diluted and taken over by the idea of only global. In terms of feminism the post modernity has provided an opportunity to enlarge prospects of all round development. The post modernity is not a historical phenomenon rather it is a "state of mass mood" framed on the effect of numerous factors some being explosion of information and knowledge, and other US sponsored purely politico-commercial liberalization. These global currents have deeply shaken the established authorities of system. A tendency of interrogation swept the mind of postmodern youth because of that they find no scope to accommodate with people of modernist bent of mind. The stance of discomfiture is more apparent in feminist affairs which for Kamala Das are platform to celebrate her victory. She has battled with open mind against socio-domestic barriers with an intention to sort out differences and reach a consensus whence onward feminism could move uninterruptedly. It is an age where Kamala Das as a flag bearing author is in a position to form an aesthetic kingdom of their own. The corner stone of this monarchy is laid down by women not only for feminist welfare but for wellbeing of humanity at large. The element motherhood governs Kamala Das in taking final decision of feminity.

The very first poem in this chapter is "Women's Shuttle" discussing monotony prevalent in Indian women's shuttle like life. They are confined to certain places like puppet. Now break is obvious "there are no longer / Any homecomings." Homecoming signifies monotony of centuries old custom put on the mind of women. Rooted evils in memory Kamala Das plans to alter by postmodern options which include global freedom and exposure. Kamala Das reiterates:

> No,
> I cannot recollect the face
> Of the man who told me he loved

My property....................
I see only those faces that
Have returned to dust..................

Mens's faces gone to dust denote defeat of male mentality which the author visualizes disappearing giving room for feminist victory. The author recalls her fifteen years old son as a sing of victory of motherhood. Between motherhood and existential nothingness women fly like shuttle but, after a long contention she has perched on the fertile and humane land of motherhood. "According to Jane-Levis, feminism has also experienced what is in fact on historical tension between a organization and practice that starts from women's claims as mothers and one that believed that main task to be the problem of defining and obtaining equality for women as individuals in the public sphere."[1] Although mother has got meaning for society but Kamala Das yet laments the shuttling life style of women as attributes this life as "A Cask of Nothing." The present poem underscores public opinion about women as an empty cask filled with nothingness. The gloomy words of author unveil underlying pain:

If I close my eyes I see nothing .
If I shut my ears I hear nothing

By closed eyes and ears she can see and hear a lot of things provided her life has individual existence and social recognition. But what dwells is "an ache within" originated from loneliness, frustration and dejection of kith and kins. Jane Freedman argues that, "men refuse to see women as total, separate human being and define them instead in terms of how they benefit men's lives. In terms of sexuality this means that women are not seen as individuals who want to share equality in the sex act."[2] The sex act sans individuality and free choice is imposed masculine task enhancing the burden of nothingness and marginality. This pressure Kamala Das attempts not only to reduce but completely eradicate as it abolishes feminist share in domestic domain. The poem that follows is "Summer - 1980" the catchword of the poem is "destruction" of old fences of masculine dominance on women's life. Like an over-vigilant fighter Kamala Das does not allow even a bit of negligence to enter her life. She asserts her standpoint boldly, "Prickly mantle called kill, kill/ all that was till a while ago,/ so dear so beautiful, yes./ Perhaps the malevolent / Alchemy of the city air/ Aided us.............." The alchemy of city air has turned gold into lead and vice versa. The city people are assumed to be rational and civilized in comparison to not-city residents. But what they did as response to feminist warfare is disparagingly hopeless.

"Caressing hands unshaped the clay ....formed a death head." The factual analysis reveal very bleak picture of feminism in cities where well-to-do and educated people dwell:

> The ideal populance for totalitarian state is a faceless and voiceless one that will carry order without a murmur. Silence is thus, a pre condition for such as government or its authority is threatened. This is Akhmotova's unpardonable fault: she was born with a voice while the state wanted her to be mute. When she spoke she was heard and supported by millions.[3]

The authority of state, society and family primarily run by male sentiment does not tolerate even just and democratic voice of women. The blind and merciless suppression of women Kamala Das and Anna Akhmatova strongly protested with a blueprint in hand for future course. In the course of battle their life is always scared of death engineered by challenged authorities of subjection.

The impact of philosophical atmosphere is evident on Kamala Das's poems as the first line of "Life's Obscure Parallel" tells, "life's obscure parallel is death". In reality there is no life without fear of death. In terms of material life the author is obsessed with victory shadowed by defeat and love covered by hatred. Having a series of contrasts she has launched her war against male maneuvering. She philosophizes the surface facts in a catching manner:

> Inside
> My throat the inward breath combats the outside
> one. And sights, see, reside not outside
> But within.

The smallest cells of her body and personality are obtained from sweet and sour experiences she has been passing through. Again Kamala Das offers her observations of herself:

> The built-in terrors of my mind
> Swoop down on me from the treetop at dusk and in
> The kitchen's unlit corners large bird of pre
> Perch with rustling claws and an all - knowing gaze.

The spontaneous terror as the part and parcel of women's life get intensified the moment "bird of prey" start hovering over her head with "an - all - knowing gaze". The disparity existent between meek wife and hunting husband is the basic cause of conflict. The racous sound of preying bird dominates the "baby - cry" which author wants to enhance by developing friendly atmosphere in family. The total life of the poet mother Kamala Das has found as a source of welfare of family and her son, but what in return she found from husband is disgust and insulting treatment:

> ....a baby once in my bed for which
> Goblets of breasts swelled burdened with milk and love?
> A sudden drought seems to have settled itself down
> On the sun bleached estuaries of my blood.

Kamala Das compares her compassion and mild flow as natural as estuaries that both are on the verge of extinction because of uncompassionate and fierce sunlight of masculinity. She finds compassion and energy from nowhere else but from her grandmother. "The mother (grandmother) is seen as a source of strength, life giving and nurturing."[4] The contrasting relationship between man and woman is always bound to be that of cat and dog, exception can be found only between woman and woman (Grandmother and Kamala Das relation) which provides energy, sympathy and support.

In the total literary output of Kamala Das "death" has been treated differently at various junctures. Life is always shadowed by death which is mediocre in its occurrence is the theme of next poem "Death Is So Mediocre". The initial wording of the poem - "life has lost its clear outline .... I may have gone half-blind" powerfully suggests that demarcation line between life and death is thin. The glamour and glow of life has gone stolen from the eye of the author. The night darkness is a time to conceal garbage from view whereas the "wrappers off many a guilt remains/ a dubious ally". The night and day, life and death are all on a dubious alliance which the poem wants to tear. By breaking the dirty knot of life and death Kamala Das wants to rectify what is proper path for common men to walk and which one to avoid. The understandable division of time is day and night (symbol of good and evil) whereas:

> All the rest are lying morgued
> With that hazy past. And, yet invitations
> Come from strangers who proudly string me between
> Starched serviette blooms at their tables.

The present is spent discussing hazy past in most individual's life. The mystery of life and attributes are difficult to tell says Kamala Das: "When asked/ to speak I find my poor mouth turn into an/ open cavern, ransacked bare ...." The unspeaking condition of the author convey impregnate nature of life of which we are part. Whatever attributes and materials one has gathered in life as facilitators have become ".....suddenly wealth and lust seem like / Languages once learnt but now forgotten". The paraphernalia of life once treasured become unspeakable as garbage the moment its burden becomes unbearable. The fear of death arriving any moment makes life an experience of mediocrity.

For Kamala Das death is ordinary in its occurrence and its "final rites are awful and vulgar". The moment of death shows "the slow unwrapping of the carcass, / the many paltry, human details that must disgust/ The esthete, the flabby thigh, the breasts that sag/ the surgery scar." During life time these organs have special meaning for esthetes and lovers but death has rendered them as disgusting object fit for quick burial.

The dilemma of death and life has been very breath suspending for the author, like T.S. Eliot she also feels "Life in death and death in life" melodrama as a part of her life. She is badly nauseated of her married life as frustrated one says, "I shall go too in silence leaving not / Even a finger print on this crowded earth." In the big crowded earth she does not want to leave even a tiniest mark of acquaintance because of total lack of genuine love. She even wants to take "away my bird - in - flight voice" because of that there developed "hundred misunderstanding that destroyed / My alliances with you and you and you........"

In the final stage of creative career Kamala Das have developed philosophical and seer's vision even in the matters of worldly and material affairs. Some time the mood of total renunciation prevails as the previous and present poem "A Journey with No Rerun" offer. The "desire" exists in the mind of the author like a "dolphin" that floats and sinks at times. The body can quit soul but desire cannot, she feels "My limbs are tense with embarrassment." She does not want to perpetuate her attachment with "you" because of her revolting temperament. Her relation with husband has been unrepairable, "I long to put aside my sacred vows/ and long to forget the sweet domestic part." Her path is parted away form that of family and world. She gladly admits herself to be amnesiac, not knowing anything of past relation. Her journey has taken different course that cannot return to its place of origination. The fury of Kamala Das goes beyond limit:

> ....the fire that I bear to warm your bed to night
> Would burn down the ramparts of my home....

She does not want any kind of compromise with her family members on the cost of her ideology and way of life highlighting self-respect and identity. These factors constitute the foundational backbone of feminist aesthetics which contemporary better-halves wish to constitute in the competent leadership of Kamala Das.

She has investigated factual and fictional realities pertaining to feminist life. The poem now under analysis "At Chiangi Airport" tells reality of Kamala Das's life at home and abroad. The poem begins with "And" that shows author's unreasonable connectivity with her painful past. She does not want to perpetuate her sorrowful days of past into present which is but extension. "travel light, / forgetting in the most convenient device of all". Life of Kamala Das is a heap of sorrow and gloom piled one on the other making it heavy burden. The facts of Chiangi airport in Singapore tell internal contrast of Kamala Das's life :

> The airport unveiled death's lustrous chamber,
> Silent acres of pearl grey wool wearying the ankles
> Like sand, arrows making out the legitimate
> gates and the shuttered illegitimate.

The open gate reality that is transparent and plain life of Kamala Das is markedly different from "shuttered illegitimate" facts of society which does not coincide and endorse the standpoint of the author. This contrast between author's view of life and that of entire society render the airport gate as "death's lustrous chambers". The airport symbolizes the gateway of lustrous world with which Kamala Das an independent seeker of dignified existence cannot harmonize. Those who have lost their memory of past can adjust with the present. She comments ironically:

> Insomniacs
> ride the escalators of the night and from within
> their fevered brains the telephone trill. Midnight gates
> rock the ocean's floor. In the cellars of the sea
> all treasure chests lie emptied.

The world of glow and glamour attracts those who are cursed with short memory, the author has capability to relate and rotate past with present and future and reverse in order to derive logical conclusion for life ahead. As she has under taken an Olympian task of paving the highway of aesthetics for postmodern women hence her conclusions must be well conceived. The point of author's worry is that a good number of young women are misguided by the facy allurements of materials. She expresses her discomfort in following lines:

> A displaced generation
> must find its comfort in tea. Fifty and two is
> not a nice age to. And, yet poetry sought
> me out one day, a pursuer, hot and painting
> and that odd glass shoe........so dainty - wonder of wonders.
> Did fit my calloused foot?

"Comfort in tea" echoes T.S. Eliot's phrase in "Prufrock ...." that we have measured our lives in "Coffee spoons" both are indicative of modern man's inclination towards trifle materialism. In such an atmosphere of suffocative and boring locale Kamala Das has sorted out the way:

> I learn to forget
> You, forget the glitter, forget the blue, forget
> the brief hope, forget the ache, forgetting is still
> the wisest move of all..........

By forgetting experiences of sweet and sour nature, she opens new path for her community that is free from partiality and greed. Kamala Das's work and that of Anne Sexton's "shows an awareness of the methods by which women are brainwashed by patriarchy, the way they internalize male norms and attitudes, deliberately ignoring their own gender and its special needs."[5]

"Death" has been very preferred subject of feminist authors. Kamala Das has inspected the different corners of death to bring out scope of life is the theme of "If Death is Your Wish". In case one prefers death over life as Kamala Das and Sylvia Plath did then killing becomes an easy game" and "brand new cult" that reveals filthy nature of intimate relations. Women are easily targeted by an "uneasy era" of men who demonstrate their strength by "guns they tote." They (men) should no longer populate this earth by like minded breeds as they will spread masculine evils vehemently. So, it is better this earth be unpopulated than evil - torn maintains Kamala Das. Kamala Das's obsession with death is the outcome of her painful and gloomy past which she wants to defeat. "What stands out most is perhaps, her focus on death. Time and again her poems express a negation of life (the life social customs and institution have provided) a yearning for the oblivion of death. This could be taken as an escapists turning away form the pressures of life / choosing death as a release from the agony of existence."[6] Kamala Das's choosing of deaths is not an escapist's attitude rather a lethal blow to patriarchy which she hates and avoids to live with. Death is an extreme kind of hatred which she would like to embrace rather than compromising.

Time and again she refers to "home" a place where people feel bond of relational love is not made of bricks but of emotion and compassion of each others. The theme of "home" built on the principles of Kamala Das makes one feel death like pain the moment one is away even on a trip is the theme of "A Short Trip". The dictum that "one reaps what one sows" is no longer applicable in the changed context of society. Now "one is bound to reap what another had sown" is more pertinent especially in the case of women's predicament. Their own sins are not so deep but the sins of husband show adverse effect on the wife's life. The same idea Kamala Das conveys in a very fitting words. "While plucking flowers / one gathered with them a squirming snake." The reversal of justice in favour of male is not a recent tale, its root lies in scriptures like Bible Vedas and Quran. Evils are permanently attached to the life of women later on endorsed by classic authors of each civilization. The very notion the author claims supporting in following lines:

> the traveler by her brief absence lifts
> from other left behind the domestic
> inhibitions that plague human beings
> who have learnt to hate illogically
> both the hated and hater
> cannot ever hope to explain why.

The customs and rituals of society victimize both male and female but none of them discover elements of why. They bear accursed life blindly and illogically with out search of reasons for such archaic punishment.

Even the short trip away from home in a subject of deep anguish because the author has developed a balanced concept of home, the very idea we find debated in the poem titled "Home is a Concept". The concept of home changes from occasion to occasion. Once Kamala Das carrying a heavy luggage was to board an aeroplane. She then had a briefcase studded with papers to be read at seminar, passport and visa and photographs of laughing children. Along with these nostalgic items she possessed "the heaviest luggage they tote in pain." In the life of the author most remarkable asset is pain of being woman that completely changed her course of life. Home is a very tender and elegant experience cannot be known from materialistic or parochial point of view:

> If home is a concept
> They shall not know It, if home is a group prepared
> to love, the traveler has not known that group and
> never shall.

Those who are away from home of their dream feel the pangs of separation. Otherwise Kamala Das and like minded women had very bitter taste of home. "The wanted speak in / strident voices" change the basic concept of home from heaven to inferno of punishment. The silence if ever prevails in such home it "holds terror" of mortuary. The average women hanged in between home and anti-home have no statement about "Commonwealth Literature" or "Nuclear Holocaust" or any other issue of larger significance. They are grinded under the load of endless domesticity. Their main concern is to beg for love, "love me, I am not so different from the ones you seem to love".

Love is a thing that makes life of an individual and home worth living otherwise it is mere storehouse of materials likely to rot soon. Meena Surjeet Singh, observes the nature of Kamala Das's love poems, "her love poems take the reader through roller - coaster journey of passionate, lusty, interludes with their attendant betrayal that always ends in failure to achieve spiritual communion."[7] Variety of emotional and erotic experiences the readers go through in the poetry of Kamala Das make them thoroughly influenced. The poem "Maturity" offers the worth of life one can obtain after reading Kamala Das poems. The image of "great cities" under which flows "stoicism of sewers" present a contrast of postmodern life. Not only sewers but many such things are found beneath the glamorous front, "the rush of putrid waste, the abstract pulling down / of shades, the switch - off of curiosity." Having found curiosity switched off Kamala Das finds life fully disconnected form society. Thus there is "closure of apertures that allow the river of unhappiness to flow in / towards the heart's restive ocean ...." In the atmosphere of paradoxical society "Kamala Das's "restive ocean" is very often interrupted. She expresses her concerns in the following lines "the eyes, the ears so that the breath, inhaled yields its/ true meaning." True meaning of life lies in creating of pure socio-natural surroundings into all churning and embracing mind of the author. "What may well be worthier than life itself" is amalgamation of practical experiences rather than information provided by secondary resources for maturity of author like Kamala Das. Her concern with love is undoubtedly central of all her poems yet she "uses neither the biting social irony of Nissim Ezikiel, not the larger philosophical themes of Sri Arvindo, or of even of Tagore but she is not totally alienated from the Indian landscape or into social milieu like well - known expatriates Dom Moraes or Tilottama Rajan"[8] Her poetry is a balanced mixture of social, political and contemporary issues and above all sentimental aspects of deprived feminity.

She has very deep and humanistic understanding of familial relationship no matter the relation is passively operational or otherwise. The notion finds poetic voice in "My Sons" where she investigates her natural bond with her sons. Love has many colours and tastes, in defining mother - son love she tells, "I used up / My blood as ink to praise its worth." Use of blood denotes sacrifices made by mother in making son full grown person. She is curious to know:

> Where is he now? Who remembers the smell
> Of his skin or the words he murmured in
> My ears? My sons are old enough to forget
> The lullabies I sang and the prayers

Tendering motherly love to sons is quite natural for Kamala Das but does not support any patriarchal ill - practices towards women no matter it be done by her sons. In the character of sons she finds dormant element of exploitative patriarchy which Kamala Das always has been fighting. She hopes her sons would also develop as monstrous males "swinging round and round with the females of their tribe." Mother poured her blood and love in the development of sons but they grew on father's pattern of blood sucking. The generation after generation devouring sons would be growing to use women of their tribe for their lusty needs. The author wants a relationship between man and woman of new generation to be based on equality, love and mutual understanding which in the present context seems impractical, therefore she has decided to part her ways from customary familial relationships. The loneliness Kamala Das suffered was an occasion of self - inspection and fresh path breaking as she feels, "at the age of 19 she suffered a nervous breakdown as a 'neglected wife' and that she was commanded to live all alone in a closed room with sunshine peeping through window."[9]

The value of relations is very precious in the entire writing of Kamala Das. Even her attachment with humanism is of exceptional category which readers find in the poem "Delhi - 1984 " the year India witnessed P M Indira Gandhi's assassination and mass carnage, murders and arsons that engulfed entire country against Sikh community under the management of white-collar criminals. They did not spare even old feeble women and school going adolescent girls. The Delhi then was set on blaze of demonic fire targeting fairs and fouls alike.

In the history of India turbans (Sikh) have set highest example of sacrifice in maintaining India as it is now. But they were brutally murdered by so called pro-Indira Gandhi white - collar criminals for the crime they did not commit. Kamala Das as a sensitive and nationalist woman was shocked to see whatever followed after PM's assassination by fanatic Sikh gaurds which was no way the deed of all community. "The long limbs / broken and bunched to seem like faggots." When dead bodies were handed over the respective families, especially wife got fainted. Not only "dead bodies" of the earning members were cause of women's swoon but those bloody gang of "tabooed arms" that brought bodies' home ware scarier. In the observation of Kamala Das religious and political fanaticism is a opium dose leading society into absolute rule of anarchy that India suffered in 1984 after Indira Gandhi's assassination. She criticizes the practice, "the scriptural / chant sounded like a lunatic's guffaw"; No divine power would like to accept these anti - social elements as follower of God's ethics. A new cult of bloodshed has started on the soil of India in which innocents were victimized only on the pretext of group identify. Heinous offence did then was hard to be seen in future again:

> No breast was left
> Unfolded, no ripe cunt overlooked
> As terror fleet of foot, did rampage

> The sedate suburbs, while in the queen's
> Funeral pyre the embers lay cooling.

One hand silent and peaceful lives were blood-washed on the other "queen's pyre embers lay cooling." The word queen is ironical indication to Indira Gandhi whose pyre is cooling down leaving India into a pool of bloody enmity for ever widening. The tag of feminism given to Kamala Das's poetry is not absolutely justified; she included many other contemporary issues of larger relevance in her works. "Her poetry and prose reflect her restlessness as a sensitive woman moving in the male dominated society......."[10] Her feminist concern is not narrow, it encompasses human an issues ignored by society, politics or any other agency of dominance. On this ground I want to enlarge Kamala Das's field of writing up to feminist aesthetics that included all nice traits of males and females, indiscriminately.

The brutal and banal traits of personality when practiced in real life turn it to hell. Women's life deprived of humanistic treatment is nothing but cattle's life is the theme of "Old Cattle". Kamala Das has impression of her life to be equal to the animals when she was discharged from hospital to be taken to home. The house for the author serves as a metaphor of motherly affection so long as she was bachelor, but after marriage the meaning of house was fundamentally changed to a "slaughter house" where Kamala Das as cattle bearing mark of vermillion on forehead is bound to settle for being butchered. Cattle are better in a sense that they can break rope to graze green grass but the author cannot because of being trained in customs and creeds of slavery. This tendency of slavery has rendered Kamala Das's life equal to cattle that she wants to uncoil by fighting the odds of society. The poem "The Ferry" is a celebration of author's desire to cross the rivers of husband's physicality and domesticity. She wants to be "featureless" and "blanched". Her life has been full of "salty blood with tears of prophets." Ultimate desire of women would be, according to Kamala Das to "erupt from between a barren woman's thighs."

Barrenness of women shows finish of re-productivity so that the curse of child care cannot fall upon women. The surrounding of feminist society is dominated by fatalists who do not allow normal life to women. "Obscure railway platforms" denote hustle and bustle of people where "mailbags alight." These mailbags" are women contained in wrappers of veil unidentified unless pierced by "fatalists seated on stone benches." These fatalist's are having "dead eyes as convicts" or they seem like "tombstones" gazing whoever passes through that way. The poem shows an inamicable relationship that persists for indefinite future between two genders. The fatalist's gaze poses a series of questions:

Ann Kaplan asks of postmodern concept of cinema where male gaze is focused to woman's body:

> "Is the gaze male"? She problemetizes to some extent what feminisms have accepted (at least since Laura Mulvey's important article on 'visual pleasures and Narrative Cinema') as the maleness of the camera eye that makes women into exhibitionists to be observed and displayed, 'coded for strong visual or erotic impact' so that they can be said to cannot to be looked-at-ness. This leaves the female as spectator in the position of either narcissistic identification or some kind of psychic cross dressing.[11]

In postmodern context the above article argues and the poem too that the body of women made an object of male gaze for economic or entertainment purpose. The position of father is Indian domestic system is very respectable so long as he carries on his obligatory responsibilities innately. The same father becomes demon when he comes under the negative influence of maleness. Being male is more primitive and hence barbaric because Kamala Das has practical experience of her own father's relation with mother. Her husband too became father when she bore children. The tendency of fathers are almost similar in every familial setup. His in human shadow as Kamala Das maintains hovers around the mind of wife, daughter and even grown up women of that family. The above paradigms are poetically illustrated in the poem "My Father's Death". The very first line narrates the insincerity of family and so-called friends on the death of Kamala Das's father. Many people were desirous to "get photographed with the corpse". Their shedding tears was a mere show of sympathy. Kamala Das highlights her father's royal position in his locality almost near to Vasco-de-Gama the Portuguese sailor who landed on Kappad:

> on both side of
> roads the people stood, pre - arranged
> to watch his flower bedecked
> hears pass and the police with polished
> batons directed the traffic orchestra.

The funeral convoy was only attended by males the female community even bereaved mother and daughter Kamala Das were restricted by custom not to be part of wailing precession. Her mother was too weak to weep normally to whom Kamala Das was to support emotionally. Time around father's death for Kamala Das and her family had been impatient punishment. Her observation of that scene of death is very awe provoking:

> He had shrewdly traded in
> his pain for a coma that was thick like a fog. He was
> like a puppet attached to its strings. The rubber tubes
> grew like tubes from every orifice and from within
> his chest a strange beast howled and moaned in pain.

Even father on deathbed could not arouse emotional feelings in the mind of Kamala Das. She attributes father with "strange beast" and "puppet" that reveals Kamala Das's derogatory attitude towards father. Mother has closely watched and witnessed father's pain and moan that disturbed her mental peace from the root. Domestic servants and neighbours have their version of meaning and effect of Kamala

Das's father's death. Children's memory being short is likely to forget father's death as she utters, "children are sculptures that soon forget their sculptor." Kamala Das's feminist concern was not taken as pro-family repute by father so "she brought shame" to family. Father's dying posture was something Kamala Das dared loving. "Only in that last coma did he seem close to me, and / I whispered into his ears that I loved him, although bad............" Kamala Das-a woman, a daughter, a wife, a mother was bad and from that point of view all males were bad no matter what domestic relations they have. Kamala Das's larger perspective of "love" encompasses those relations whom she hated strongly "in the task of loving the bad ones were the ablest." Kamala Das as a daughter has always starved of fatherly love:

> You should have hugged me father
> just once to your breast, you should
> have used kind words
> at least once a year
> you gave my sons hundred rupees note
> you purchased their devotion but my
> price was too high for you,
> your wallet could not hold abstract
> currency ....

She was not satisfied with the kind of formal relation father had with Kamala Das. Her social field activities were painful to father as it all brought defamation to the family. The expansion of feminist knowledge is not accepted as natural even in the phallocentric society. Meena Alexander has rightly remarked of the widening gap between male and female relationship of knowledge sharing:

The woman writer had to cut through the bonds of feminity; those structures of patriarchal authority that seemed to stand outside her though powerfully gathered into her intimate grasp of self, even as she set out the slow and often difficult task of discovering the sources of her own genius. In a gendered world as Marry Wollstonecraft painfully discovered knowledge was never unmarked.[12]

Even natural capabilities were categorized on classes of gender which Wollstonecraft in America and Kamala Das in India strongly opposed by social opinion building. The father's death for Kamala Das is patriarchy's death as far as her domestic atmosphere is concerned. It is a lose as well as victory for Kamala Das and her victimized mother in an unconventional way. The marginalized and dehumanized life of women as Kamala Das observed is well presented symbolically in "Wood Ash." Women's life has been a green forest cut and burnt to ashes

Because of lacking of coherence and co-existential mutuality between natural counterparts. She feels herself deprived and starved of love and fellow feeling as the following lines show:

> the wild fire destroyed the flowering shrubs
> the wild fire burnt down the trees
> the wild fire burnt then itself down and in the blood of my ancestors the embers lay cooling..............

The thrice used phrase "wild fire" denotes fiery distance and dissonance existing between male and female resulting into destruction of "flowering shrubs", "burning down trees" and finally the "wild fire" itself cooling down in the ancestor's embers. Out of this chain of burning "fragrance of wood" and "smoke" surface every where. "Dravidian King" the authority of Kamala Das's family raised "loud war cry " listening which numerous beasts "cowered in fear":

> The fierce storms clawed the country's face
> The pagan danced round the flames in ritual gloom
> The chieftains bartered their kingdoms away for trinkets ....

Ancestral blood and customs have deeply but negatively imprinted on the mind of the author which finds repercussion in the form of "sea moans". Technically this poem is open ended invoking Kamala Das's nostalgic experiences in the form of "sea moan". The sea inside womenfolk is all the time wailing and roaring for the redemption from the confinement of house. The identical idea is conveyed in "The Lunatic Asylum" symbolic manifestation of women as lunatic and asylum as their domestic limitations. There is a "light" burning all through night that is "an unshaped bulb" like a "teardrop hanging from the dead while ceiling." At the same time "sun" burns from the eyes of inmates all gazing pitiless. The light of the eyes is not for illumination but for burning the objects (women in front). There is a third bulb that also burns dimly in the mind of insomniac women like a "lantern". There is a dim memory of past that dances like a ghost before women in fearful manners. All three sources of light are meant to enhance afflictions in the life of women instead of luster and gaiety. The conclusion offered therefore is:

> they were
> brave enough to escape, yes, to step out
> of the brute regimentals of same
> routine ignoring the bugles, the wail
> of sirens and the robots stern
> bark, hup two three hup two three
> hup two three................

Dance steps to which women are attuned are not suggestive of happiness but monotony of routine fixed to their life. They want to insert freshness, energy and rejuvenation in life which is not possible unless lunatic asylum is broken to pieces where they are kept for long past. The dead existence of women in conventional boundary of family is bound to lose their basic traits which were explained by romantic authors also, "..............like Dorothy Wordsworth who kept walking in the journals or Wollstonecraft's imprisoned Maria who drew inspiration from her painfully swollen breast, or Mary Shelley who in fierce. consorting acts of imagination drew on bits and pieces of dead bodies for a monster that could never be birthed."[19] All three romantic feminist authors of different cultural units have un homely realization of women's condition which they wanted to modify as Kamala Das adhered to their mode of reformative writing. Women's real speech if made so obscure that their decoding can be done by a sensitive and penetrating author Kamala Das as the poem "Speech" conveys. The hidden contents of suppressed voice can be understood by the way Kamala Das suggests:

> Lyre strings
> Earth's network of veins
> And Piano keys
> Each livened pulse;
> Wind's finger tips
> Twangs ....

These musical and natural instruments offer a note of music which are conceived of pain, and additional message that an ordinary man cannot follow so is the life of women. The rain fall, trees, and lichen convey their music in their respective vocal style. Inherent meaning of all these things are difficult to reach unless one is not well harmonized and made one with them. Similarly women's life and agony cannot be understood from man's point of view because that is conveyed in soundless speech as a premonition of "Fear". "Fear" is a small poem which communicates true mental state of mind that runs from birth till death. Fear especially of women's life is "a lidless eye" always confronting nasty happenings. Analogy is made with "a noonday sun come at last / To stay ....../ substance,/ Bereft of shadow / A scream / A Swift - knife gleam / Deafens the unwarned / human ear......" "sunlight", "a scream" , "swift - knife" and "bereft of shadow" are adjectives denoting real life of women always facing the fear. The poetry of Kamala Das discover current issues along with women's concerns as the poem "The Sea at Galle Face Green" tells. The central theme of the poem is hidden is these phrases." Did the Tamils smell so different" and "it patrolled the empty shore". Kamala Das has double curse to undergo, one that she is a woman and secondly of Tamil community (dark complexion). In Indian history Tamilians are considered inferior to the Aryans because of dark complexion in addition to that womanhood is a endless torture cell that Kamala Das has been tolerating since birth. Incessant pain blows have rendered Kamala Das's life as worthless and empty that none but only sea discharges its duty towards the author without fail.

The city Kamala Das belonged to has been resplendent once is like "half burnt corpse" and dwellers are "maimed - limbed" and the sky above is "smoke - stained". The surrounding thus created is suggestive of suffocation and boredom. Even typical vegetation (shrub Katurmuringa) is stopped of "joyous tremor while the breezes blow." Neither birds are singing nor flowers are blooming around where the Kamala Das community is destined to dwell. What dominates that locality of Tamils and Kamala Das is the stomps of boots ......worn by adolescent gunmen ordered to hate." This description leads to ethnic problem faced by Tamils is Srilanka because of Singhele's dominance there. She is shocked to face this kind of hatred between the two groups of people. "What secret chemistry let them down?" Has nature made Tamils by different clay that they are treated differently by other ethnic groups? This question of Kamala Das relates to humanity and universal brotherhood most often destroyed by cheap politicians all around the world.

In the writing of Kamala Das not only feminist problems are raised and discussed but social, cultural and civilizational points are also debated with a humanitarian attitude. Hence one can say that her concern of writing covers more deep issues than only feminist. "She believes that the poet's raw material is neither stone not clay but the poet's personality, yet the personal does not outweigh the public concern of her art"[14] Her main concern is to better public atmosphere by improving womenfolk as they are basic brick of social foundation. Only women's bettered life cannot transform the face and soul of public unless they are properly assisted by their natural counterparts.

The nation and nationality are constituted of all constituents those who are mainstream of administration and governance. How can one society be called superior over the other on the ground of face and complexion? There was fear and danger in the air "and every window was shut" in Srilanka when there was clash between Tamils and Singhalese. She presents a very dirty scene of Srilanka:

> As the copse smouldered,
> Fear and stench sweet as
> That of raw cashewnuts
> Roasting......................

The "cashewnuts roasting" denotes corpse smouldering in Srilankan streets of both warring community. The nature is performing its duty honestly towards humanity "without sign of shock or pain. It patrolled the empty shore." The empty shore is the mind of selfish people divided on the basis of class, creed, religion and language. This divisive tendency has damaged social fabric beyond repair laments Kamala Das.

Almost identical idea is continued in the poem "Smoke in Colombo". Due to long run bloodshed in Srilanka the capital city Colombo is thickly coverec by smoke of gunpowder that Kamala Das is bound to retain in mind as a sing of human tragedy. The smoke "lingering on as milk lingers on/ in udders after thecalves are buried" is an ironical rendering of Kamala Das's impression of what is happening in Colombo. The same message is repeated in following words, "lingering on as grief lingers on within women rocking emptied cradles." Entire warring society, according to Kamala Das is mad and whimsical. She does not approve disruptive tendency any kind, "a somnambulistic / Daze was in their eyes, there was no space / Between us and their Guns..........." The group of Kamala Das visiting Colombo tired of their own problems was insensate enough to understand, "fear or resist/ the abrupt moves / of an imbecile will." She has no comment to pass but that they are stupid and thoughtless manifestation of will by which no human gain can be had.

The lose of identity of contemporary women is a big concern of Kamala Das as the poem "Shopper at the Cornells Colombo" dismantles. Colombo has been a tourist destination along with a point of conflict between Tamils and Singhlese for a pretty long time. The author as a champion of universal brotherhood and love has visited Colombo where she finds her identity enmeshed with people around the shopping complex. She was seeming to be part of visited locality:

> ....in red slacks and shirt my hair
> Tied up in bandanna, my Indianness
> Concealed, I merge well with the expatriates

The Indian features of Kamala Das is hidden rather she has become native of Colombo by putting on attires that locals do. Having done purchases she was upto payment counter where salesgirls "see through my guise." The artificial concealment of identity cannot help for ever. The moment Kamala Das's distinct identity is confirmed the native people's view is quickly changed, "and their cruel mouths bleed/ when they make attempts to stab me with a smile." The customary smile of sales girls become stabbing the moment they learnt Kamala Das to be an Indian national. The point of problem for the author is that creation of universal tolerance and peace is not a cup of tea even after abolishing her national distinctions. She does not muse like a romantic or reflective author rather gives adequate focus to the problems faced by society and individuals. "The poets conveys here the power that a woman holds, and her idiom is fundamentally modernistic instead of being romantic or idealistic or in the previous age."[15] The problem confronted by Tamils in Srilanka is political and ethnic in nature that must be dealt with pure humanistic point of view rather than romantic or idealistic parameter, held Kamala Das. Ethnically Kamala Das belongs to Tamil clan which she never claimed as superior to other groups. This kind of illogical complexes become bone of contention in society that she never allowed to grow in her personality, however whenever she is maltreated on that illogicity she feels hurt. She argues in the following poem "After July" these points in detail. The month of July was the deadline after that Tamils cannot be allowed to stay in Colombo. With ban on Tamils in Colombo, the whole city looked like a desert because, "no flower sellers / came again to the door with strings / of jasmine to perfume the ladies hair." The Tamils were beautifiers of Srilankan women by selling jasmine flowers but ethnically they were treated as "other" unifit in the society of Sri Lanka. They flew from the streets of Colombo after July. The Tamils were in fear deprived of their original temperament. "Their smell began to resemble the rats / A mixture of dung by all Singhlese." Kamala Das compares the internal conflict of Sri Lanka with that of Jews and Christians during Second World War. The ethnic hatred of two warring community goes to the extent of killing smaller children. Kamala Das laments that state:

> Flitter rose from the dead, he demanded
> ....he hailed,
> The robust Aryan blood, the sinister
> Brew that absolves a man of his sins and
> Gives him right to kill his farmer friends
> The dark Dravinian laid his three year old child
> On his Lap Little mother, he cried, close you eyes
> and sleep.

The last sentences manifest fanatic level of ethnic hatred which does not spare a three year child even before crying mother. The society bereft of "innocence" is worst than hell and on such places talk of love and brotherhood is a joke. In these poems Kamala Das is cut free from erotica, she now bothers larger problems society has been facing for long past. Hence Kamala Das discuses "the aesthetic order ....never strayed too far from their origins in daily life or the values of communal existence."[16] The existence of community and that of individual is reciprocal and both jointly can forge out a aesthetic system allowing all to survive amicably in the socio - political and domestic domain of the author. But what she finds in the life of women is that" A Certain Defect in the Blood"? Which does not let women assert their existential freedom? The central thesis of the poem is "It was a defect/ In our blood that made us the land's inferiors / A certain muddiness in the usual red..........." The genetic weakness rooted in blood finds manifestation in outer behavior of women is the basic cause of suffering in this world. The feminist movements in India and abroad are eclipsed by "fear" that hinders culmination:

> Like spiders exposed
> To a water jet we curled ourselves into
> Tight balls, preparing to escape, to escape
> Into sleep and its wide freedoms of the soul.

The "wide freedoms of soul" women can never enjoy because of half hearted participation in liberation movement that is scared by fear of defeat. Even emerging new generation of girls are taught to live in thereat and skepticism of their potentiality. Kamala Das uses image of a "flying plane" denoting the vastness of sky for women where they can demonstrate their inherent energy of mind and body. Thus "their hopes reviving for a moment or two" but suddenly their mind turns down because of certain defect in blood. Women suffer a lot because of such defect and search for a "kinder country their stigma / Might stay unrecognized.........." The possibility of finding a such country where women's stigma is unrecognized is practically romantic utopia. Kamala Das bitterly depreciates escapanist attitude of women. She backs up women of today to take field with a determined mind to win and settle score with arch enemy. In this way they can build their tower of existence and assert aesthetic norms. Destructive tendency of men can be well substituted with creative and all - embracing traits of better halves. The social fabric prepared by positive and creative threads of women would be better place to live. A,

Ayappa Panicker in the introduction of N.V. Raveendran's book *The Aesthetic of Sensuality* comments on major contents of Kamala Das's writing:

> The uniqueness of Kamala Das among Indian English poets perhaps, is that she is the least academic of them, either in attitude or by training. Nissim Ezikiel, Ramanujan a trained linguist, Parthsarthy a teacher/ editor, Jayant Mahapatra, Shiv K. Kumar, Arvind Mehrotra etc are professional academic, Kamala Das being largely self - taught, the impression a reader has is that she draws her inspiration from life rather than library.[17]

The inspiration Kamala Das draws from life is more valid and reliable than life - information collected from book - shelves by her contemporaries. Hence her draft of life aesthetics is more practical and realizable and her suggestions to resolve man-woman conflict more handy. The poem that follows is "Toys" revealing true evils in the male mind. "...........new race of men who arrive / with patriotic slogans to sow dead seeds." Dead seeds are old customs that are likely to grow in the practice of men and women. "The womb weeps blood" because the seed inside womb is male originated and oriented hence fit to termination maintains Kamala Das.

> How much kinder to remove this outdated
> Growth, to bury it inside the earth and let
> The maggots breed in its hollow than let it
> Remain in the worthless
> Body of a toy.

Women's body is a toy which is cursed to contain contagious seed of maleness for future expansion that Kamala Das wants to curve immediately. A stage of verbal impotency has come in the poetic career of Kamala Das where "words are Birds" that have flown away. The wings of imagination are tired unable to undertake any adventure. "Dusk is upon my hair / Dusk is upon my skin", feels Kamala Das. She is so tired of battling life that she utters words of fatigue and despair "I am not sure / that I shall see / The blessed dawn again." This is a temporary phase in the life ot author very soon to be altered into new morning of feminist celebration.

As an activist for the welfare of women and down trodden Kamala Das has fought legislative election in which she was beguiled by her so-called supporters. She had a bitter experience of political election-engineering particularly for a female contestant having marginal financial support. The poem "Honour" offers a realistic picture of election scene in which women, wealth, wine, muscleman, corrupt methods and hypocrisy are applied as basic ingredient of Indian democratic system. Dalit Pather party candidate came to seek Kamala Das's blessing for electoral victory in a non - democratic manner as if blessing is a thing that can be snatched away. "Wearing a rude skull cap .... a bandage round his arm." This look of Pather Party supporters was not hypocritical but genuine. They are musclemen campaigning by way of physical strength showing their open desire of victory by hook or crook. Grassroot men are silent devoid of their democratic demands bound to cast vote in the favour of more crowdy political party candidate. In such an anarchic condition Kamala Das felt seriously embarrassed and hopeless as far as common people's welfare and honour is concerned. She by her own experiences presents the condition of battling women with family, husband and her physicality :

> Who can muzzle me, born out of that uneasy soil nourished
> By sweat, semen, blood, the juices of placenta and the strangled babe?

At national level in the name of democratic practice common men are largely cheated so are women mistreated no matter what social status and caliber they enjoy. In the name of honour they are dishonoured every moment in the hands of intimate relatives, "Honour was a plant my ancestors watered/ In the day, a palm to mark their future pyre / At night their surfs / Let them take to bed their little nieces, and pregnancy." What is meaning of honour for a woman in family and that for common man in Indian democratic system can be understood in the light of prevalent paradoxes of social, political and familial system.

Illegitimate pregnancy is a blot on the face of man-woman relationship which nature has created for better mutual understanding and sharing of love-bond. This kind of undesired pregnancy is "thrown into wells and ponds / From which they rose like lotuses and water lilies each with / A bruise on her throat............ ."This description in indicative of suffering of women under the garb of fake familial honour so is suffering lot of common man under the coverage of democracy. What happens in reality is a joke:

> Today they laugh at laws, that punished
> no such only the poor
> Were ravished, strangled, drowned, buried
> behind snake shrine
> Cheated of their land, their huts and hearths;
> oh the poors were
> Laugh-raisers such comedians on the lush
> lush stage of that
> feudal age..........

Kamala Das comments drastically that feudal age is not yet passed away it has only changed its face. Women and common electorals are treated as slave and colonized entity fit to be used as per need of feudal mentality of opportunist leader so the strategy of deception goes uninterrupted in out society by the authorities that Kamala Das wants to control by creating awareness in exploited group of people. In political and social spheres women have found prejudiced representation as Linda Hutcheon observes:

> ....it is certainly demonstrable that both feminism and postmodernism are part of same general crises of cultural authority, as well as part of a more specific challenge to the notion of representation and its address, there is a major difference of orientation

> between the two that cannot be ignored : we have seen that postmodernism is politically ambivalent for it is double coded - both complicitous with and contesting of cultural dominants within which it operates, but on the otherside, feminisms have disdinct unambiguous political agenda of resistance.[18]

The distinction between post modernity and feminism as Linda Hutcheon cited is yet more clarified by Kamala Das's next poem "Daughter of the Century" is which an individual woman's stigma and that of entire female group is exposed in front of society at large. We (females) are expert in copying the manners of colonizers as birds and beasts do of their ancestors doing. Hence qualitatively we are close to animals living on the group identity and behaviors. The city we live as a place of rationality and individualism kills our distinctive features of individuality, "the city crushes its inhabitants." There is two side eradication of feminist identity first by surrounding and then by women by themselves:

> We ate our forefathers
> To gather the vigour of living
> Out grand children shall perhaps eat us
> When their turn arrives.
> ....
> We mated like Gods but begot only our killers.

The process of identity formation and life extinction lies in our own character which even God cannot prohibit. Each mother begets her killer by breast feeding. We all are own enemy by spreading hatred, jealousy and imbecility. The sum of our social projection as Kamala Das observes is, "..................little wrecks at the basement of sea / one wreck examining the other with a fault - finding eye." One blind is showing the way to other blind is the tale of all people in this world. In a general statement Kamala Das cites "This is a world pickled well in brine / A world we intend to save for a rainy day." The devastating nature and man's attitude towards himself is not different in intention as both destroy themselves. "Yet death promotes a kind of life" that is more meaningful than monotonous life which has not tasted the bitterness of circumstances. We originate from death circumstances again heading for death. "We are aided by death in out careers" sums up Kamala Das as the total essence of life. "At night the hunter and the hunted often lie asleep / In an innocence shared unwittingly." The conditions of life and its prey the man is always face to face and "what is real is what we see / The child following wood duck's tail...... ." The child life is a wild goose chase resulting into nothingness that is frustration and pessimism opines Kamala Das. In utter meaninglessness of life the author recalls her husband and asks "have I met you in real life too, or are you just a symbol?" Husband is not only relation but a symbol of domestic and familial authority that plans to kill counterpart. "The poetry of Kamala Das has been hailed as an excellence because of the apparent imaginative daring, stylistic innovation, richness of energy, and music. All these qualities emerge from her poetic genius, she is a natural poet, not a semi - skilled craftsman trying to construct poetic artifacts."[19]

In the light of above statement the following poem "The First Meeting" can be analyzed as not only a meaningless cavalcade of protesting woman author but a thoughtful and logical author's artistic presentation. Her first meeting with her husband / lover was never a pleasant and rememberable experience. Both were average man and woman however the emotional and customary gap that existed between them was unbridgeable. She as a woman of hopes and aspirations was expecting to be loved and welcomed by the husband but what she encountered was "fragile comeliness". All cities which Kamala Das dwelt has been enlivened by the beauty of female body and mind as the author recalls:

.......For I had seen
On posters spanning the widest streets of
Every city that I lived in, only
A giantess, protector of myriad

Destinies, holding things together
With weathered hands, one who wore on her face
The features of an entire land.

The contributive presence of female beauty can be realized in every field of human life. The posters in streets, houses, offices, and roads are well dominated by women's active presence that cannot be substituted by any other means claims the author. However when she faces her husband in the game of love she finds herself in a miserable condition. The natural propensity of women is to be fully honest in matter of love:

I never knew any
Politics, Wielded no religion or
Caste to empower my claims; yes, never
Feared calumny, poverty, pain or death.

But her transparent simplicity of dedication to love has been considered characteristic weakness, that opinion Kamala Das dislikes. Husbandial reluctance "unnerved me" says Kamala Das in the moments of intimacy. Traditionally women feel protected under the hoary shadow of male's but internal reality is different. The kind of love the author is destined to receive from her husband is no way better than the dangers inflicted by the outsider. The irony of every woman is inexplicable hold Kamala Das by her own love experiences. Jane Freedman puts the same idea in very clear way:

> Women's lack of control over their bodies and sexualities is for, feminists, a part of man's domination of women. For some feminists sexuality and other issues surrounding are less central to women's oppression than other economic, or political factors for others, sexuality is the very key to men's domination of women.[20]

Biological and psychological makeup of women's personality and body condition their subjection by the hand of men. The points raised in this poem are continued in "The Sensuous Woman Ill". The social systems have categorized women even in the matter of illness and physical needs. "Women must choose their illness as she / chooses her clothes to suit her style." This is not author's advice but direction of social customs especially for women. In order to win sympathy, love and mercy woman's falling ill in a particular way is must otherwise they cannot get adequate familial attention. Her morbidity as Kamala Das points out can create friendly atmosphere:

> So that she may lie,
> A martyr's halo
> Lighting up her pillowcase, under rugs
> Of cashmere, or silken quilts, limbs flaccid
> As a body's kin cool a rose ....

These attributes of a wailing woman can be of good help as far as her relation's is concerned. People may visit her with flower and fruit to offer. Her place of sickness will be well cared of with variety of things that show her social and individual status. In the period of sensuous woman's sickness some people do not fail to see even eroticism:

> ....bare of such exotica /, and must stoop
> To kiss the back of an idle hand, unused
> To chores all except that of kindling love,
> And as day and night as one tie after
> Another roll away and ocean's vast
> Languour seizes her blood ....

The point underlying this description exposes that bed ridden woman is not sick but those who come to console her are mentally sick of sexuality. There is a conflict between masculine and feminine attitude of existence and identity. Kamala Das concludes this poem with a note of philosophy:

> The state of life and death fade, and nailed
> To the pleasant cross of Being she staddles
> The handless clockface of eternity.

The "pleasant cross of Being" that is temporal and time bound existence is contrasted with "handles clockface of eternity" which is eternal and a final search of Kamala Das as a human being. Her attempt to formulated feminist aesthetics for contemporary women in unfriendly atmosphere gets energy from the same source of resistance. As a poet she places her practical experiences over linguistic signs as they are only manifestations not reality. The poem under scrutiny "The Word Is Sin" is a supporter of my view. Words have their limitation as far as expression of mind currents and physical agonies are concerned. The "world is nothing better nothing worse." Kamala Das does not expect any more from works she uses for revealing herself. The bitter physical and mental experiences Kamala Das and other women have gone through cannot be expressed better than felt on mind:

> Women brooding in cancer wards
> Remembering more than all
> Their new kitchen sinks
> Branded cattle on their last long walk
> ....
> And children's blood on zebra - crossing

These experiences cannot be communicated appropriately in terms of linguistic and objective-co-relatives. All great poets have felt language's impotency as far as powerful rendering of heart felt experiences, pains and pleasures are concerned. Readers are well aware of Kamala Das's fascination for home where love and comeliness awaits earnestly for family member. It is obsession with Kamala Das to recall home frequently in order to find consolation, peace, love and satisfaction. As she utters here:

> Home is what we return to battered by work

Illness or love,
Home is where the dreams awaits us
And knife sharpened for the kill
Home is where the god who failed us stands awaiting
And his name is sin
Nothing better, nothing worse.

Home is a place of divergent experiences blended together and one can make sense of it the way one attends it. Kamala Das has all sweet and sour experiences attributing the totality of home. She finally reaches a conclusion that whatever be the tastes of home it is all a subject of experience at personal level than linguistic representation. Women's position in Indian society is hinted at as origin of sin which Kamala Das and Stevie Smith explored in their respective national and cultural units; "she (Stevie Smith) voices her protest against patriarchal order in a very subtle and civilized manner. There is a genteel quality about Smith's poetry which speaks volumes for the culture she was groomed in, the culture she knew she had to conform to in order to survive in a world that was indifferent to women's aspirations."[21]

Different symbols are used by Kamala Das to express her disgust for conventional mode of life of which people boast highly. Social and economic system we support and stay with is parasitic and prone to crumbling as the first line of the poem "The House-Builders" reveals. "The cicadas in brambled foliage / naturally concave. So also these men." As insects make their houses inside the tree stem so are big people in the so called civilized society. Their high position is a big joke that can crumble on the blow of wind. Theoretically Kamala Das was in favour of economically weaker section of society who elevate "alien rich" by their manual work. Those elevated alien rich throw ugly names to these people by "Telgu film songs". They are not given any credit for what they did in the larger welfare of society. The heroes of society (rich and high) are indebted of poor men's extraordinary doing. The gap existent between rich and poor cannot be filled in by any attempt of government and the difference can be high lighted by the life styles; "but past sunset / their best sound ribalds, their lusts seem robust." These so called prosperous men are "puny, toy men of dust" having neither mental not physical endurance. Their glamour is showy, insubstantial and parasitic hence unreliable. On the other side dust ridden downtrodden group of people despite economic crisis have strength to endure natural and systemic onslaught. The opinion applies to womenfolk in a limited sense as they too are side lined from the mainstream of family and society, still they endurantally live.

The poetic excursion of Kamala Das has to conclude here as the poem "The Ferry Hour" hints. All her endeavours favouring human welfare specially women's have achieved some target yet not fully. Nature has ever served as powerful metaphor for Kamala Das's mental equivalent:

> Yes, the trees are being erased now.
> And the bright sea lassoing the shore
> The hill paling in the blue, the birds
> Hiding in the bough, the cow, the dog
> Beside the door............

In the poetry of Kamala Das five basic elements, earth, water, fire, air, sky the total constituents of physicality of creatures, along with cow, dog, tree and birds have vital contribution in making of larger personality of author. All these natural objects have formed a contour of face in front of the author. The birds singing in the boughs, roaring sea have come to a halt holding the hands of Kamala Das. Some times they have served as supporters and sometimes not, they all are "sobbing beside my bed." The ultimate message of this poem is that these conducive and sometime unfriendly forces are getting ferried from physical entity to internal ocean of author's memory. She concludes by saying, "it is the ferry hour at last, "The poet's memory is presented in the following words:

> Like bales, and bales of bleached white cotton

I shall stack my thoughts on the boats dark floor
With chilling finger tips I have erased
Even the face with its weeping eyes
On the laundered sheets of memory.
I shall squate all night to reach that shore.

By erasing the folded corners of memory Kamala Das wants to cross the ocean to reach that shore where she is winner having defeated all discordant forces. One can notice in this description an element of escapanist's attitude very often found in Keatsian romanticism but it would be unfair because Kamala Das wants only synthesis inside her personality which has been battling all through. M.K. Naik's reading of Kamala Das is commendable "Many of Kamala Das's love poems have Browningesque dramatic quality. Like Browning's women her persona sees herself in different situations against a concrete background, reacting to incidents in the development of soul."[22]

Memory serves in the poetry of Kamala Das as a bridge connecting past with the present it may be of any nature. "My Mother at Sixty Six" is a poem based on dramatics of memory that assists the author to live her present loaded with energy. Now the author has a trip into past with her grandmother who appears "doze, open mouthed her face ashen like that / of a corpse and realized with pain / that she was as old as she looked." Sudden shock of concrete reality brings Kamala Das back to present where she notices, "Trees sprinting, the merry children spilling / out of their home." These are the indicators of optimism Kamala Das presently enjoys only on the tinge of grandmother's memory. After airport checkups at Cochin she gets lost in the past of her grandmother. "I looked again at her wan, pale / as a late winter's moon, and felt that old familiar ache." In the life of women common feature of pain can be found any where that a sensible woman Kamala Das can better understand. While bidding farewell to grandmother she kept-smiling, smiling and smiling only on the behalf of grandmother's memory.

This chapter's final but no way least poem "The Annamalai Hills" is a premonition of a series of ten poems composed on author's Aunamalai experience. In the infinite body of nature the poet and her poetic explorations have very tiny share. The nature's working is spontaneous feels Kamala Das "no clock's here at Aunamalai" yet surrounding natural events happen timely and punctually. What miracle is at work the author wants to discern. One "muezzin's call from cold mosque" that lingers dissonantly appears harsh and unnatural to the author. She has no fascination for religious rites and rituals as an essential thing for proper social functioning. The morning clarion bird has stopped singing meanwhile "within my heart the mist ascends the / mountains awake." Awaking of mountain in the mind of observing and contemplating author is indicative of her indomitable will to win the adversities hovering the feminist life. However, along with mountain the mist also rises suggesting the perpetual conflict that runs between will power and surrounding in the mind of the author. The rift between Kamala Das and her un-friendly surrounding, poetically suggested by mountain verses mist is elaborated thus:

> It had been only the mist rising against the hill,
> clinging and unclinging as it must always do, it had
> no kinship with the hills, no blood tie it was at best
> a minor collision, nothing else.
> The mountain a metaphor of feminist victory flag
> held in the hand of the author proclaims:
> ......the mountain speak:
> I was alone, I am alone, I will be alone
> .....with the languour of queens, encient
> the fog ascends the stairways of sky.

Despite being alone, unsupported Kamala Das's will power never felt disheartened. She was betrayed, sexuality exploited and emotionally dried out by kith and kins however, "Annamalai (Kamala Das)stands undisturbed. / Wrapped in shrouds of betrayal, the woman walks alone / no longer seeking comfort - in human speech." Assurances coming out from human speech regarding feminist goodness is new cheating strategy holds Kamala Das. "The mountain seems deaf-mute, but the flesh of her spirit is but its flesh." The emotional turmoils pertaining to humanity and feminity go on perpetually in the mind of the author is well manifest in this poem.

The poem studied in the present chapter "Formation of Aesthetic Territory" is powerful evidence of author's outer and inner journey enriching her knowledge of social fabric. The war Kamala Das has launched against patriarchal practices is not for demonstration and calling attention of media but for sensitization of mass mentality against evils rampant in our society. She is not opposite to man but masculinity which is an evil no way tolerable to Kamala Das that she wants to substitute it with humanity based on mutual understanding between male and female. Energy of man's body coupled with woman's love and compassion can make this world better place to dwell. As far as erotic side of love is concerned Kamala Das never sidelines it on the pretext of private beahviour but brings to central focus as essential practice of nature which man-woman duo has to follow amicably. Kamala Das's poetry is not originated from book selves rather originates from her own physical and emotional transactions with the world, the surrounding and the relations. She is not satisfied with showing aggression against anti - feminist nature of society but she wants to weave her own social fabric on the principle of mutual love, co-existence and better emotional understanding. These elements are corner stone of her aesthetic sensibility on which society and individual can move.

References and works cited

1. Jane Freedman, *Feminism* (New Delhi: Viva Books), p. 43.
2. *Ibid,* p. 61.
3. Manju Jaidka, *Recent Trends in Woman's Poetry,* p. 109.

4. *Ibid*, p. 12.
5. *Ibid*, p. 43.
6. *Ibid*, Pp. 78-79.
7. Mina Surjeet Singh, *Six Women Poets*. (New Delhi Prestige Publication, 2003), p. 125.
8. A.N. Dwivedi, *Kamala Das and Her Poetry*, p. 25.
9. *Ibid*, p. 24.
10. *Ibid*, p. 20.
11. Linda Hutcheon, *The Politics of Postmodernism*, Pp. 146-147.
12. Meena Alexander, *Women in Romanticism* p. 4.
13. *Ibid*, p. 20.
14. Mina Surjeet Singh, *Six Women Poets*, p. 106.
15. A.N. Dwivedi, *Kamala Das and Her Poetry*, p. 69.
16. Meena Alexander, *Women in Romanticism* p. 5.
17. N.V. Raveendra, *Aesthetics of Sensuality*, (Intro. by K. Ayyappa Panicker), p. IV.
18. Linda Hutcheon, *The Politics of Postmodernism*, p. 138.
19. R. Mittapalli & Pier Paolo Picincco, *Kamala Das: A Critical Spectrum*, p. 17.
20. Jane Freedman, *Feminism*, p. 61.
21. Manju Jaidka, *Recent Trends in Woman's Poetry*, p. 69.
22. M.K. Naik, *A History of Indian English Literature*, p. 208.

Postscript

The poems put under this section are based on Annaamlai mountain that serves as symbol of indomitable will-power and long lasting endurance of women's personality. Women at large have been put on firy trial be it Sita, Savitri or Lady Lazarus or hand to mouth women at grass root level. In every trial they stood exceptionally endurant and victorious that certifies their miraculous capability to lead society to a better and balanced future. These poems are untitled yet they are called Annamalai Poems. The first poem of the series explains author's frequent visiting to the hill region's serpentine path that leads traveler to ups and downs where "tattered peasants beckoning to me." The torn flag on the peak of a cliff indicate shifting of old flag with new one. The road Kamala Das pledged to tread was not smooth and comfortable but full of tough challenges. The excursion she deliberately opted for is supported by her own body and mind that have no shelter but movement. "My poor body that had perhaps no home, / no territory to cail its own." Kamala Das attributes her journey as "somnambulistic" whose destination stands in uncertainty. Her movements in the region has been unnoticed even by tea garden labourers (Specially women) who are large in number over there. "There was none to recognize / but the birds hidden in the silver oaks / a bird that cried out my name a shrill cry, "the author's personality has been obscure in the region amongst women but a bird cried her name from silver oak symbolically exposes the sacramental nature of mission which nature supports and appreciates. The proper name gives additional value to the poem. Anamudi peak is the destination Kamala Das intends to climb up and establish feminist flag piercing the dense fog and pebbled rough path.

The second smaller poem is but extension of symbols analyzed in the first one whenever Kamala Das was covered in night of her own self she called her out to travel to destination she has decided. She bifurcates her personality into two : one, responding to the traditional values of society which intend to subjugate feminist life, two who listens to the \call of soul for a new and challenging journey. When she is awakened from the slumber she finds herself, "unaccustomed / fare for one such as I / a misfit when awake." A woman like Kamala Das born in a typical Nair south Indian family was expected to accommodate with family norms otherwise she would be called a blot and blasphemy on the pious family. These ugly names the author accepted with courage and started a journey of her own that traditional family had never dreamt of.

The outer journey of Kamala Das turns inside of soul that has been witnessing "loneliness" and "grief" for a long time past is the theme of third poem. Annamalai series of poems are wonderful combination of outer and inner topography scaled by the author emotionally well attached to her inner strength. The life of Kamala Das would have been rich in "loneliness" and "grief" that have "grown heavy as a vault one that / only death may open ...." whenever this burden is released from the head of the author she would not sense and feel it because of its ancient presence in her life. Death has been a favourite subject of Kamala Das because it is a final curtain fall on endless agonies of life. She expresses her inclination for death, "there is only one claimant whom by mistake we call death." Death is a limit reaching which Kamala Das finds life's pangs finished. We are blind followers of life that offers nothing but grief, Kamala Das advises that their's are "inadequate power to perceive beyond the farthest precincts of truth." We have contaminated view confined only upto fake pleasures of physicality that Kamala Das wants to transcend. In a metaphysical phraseology she turns her focus from celebration of body to mind and life to death as John Donne experimented and is known for:

> If only the
> Human eye could look beyond the
> Chilling flesh, the funeral pyre's
> Rapid repast and then beyond
> The mourner's vanquished stance, where would
> Death be then ....

Death and life are two distinct paradigm most often misunderstood even by wise men. What is called life is crowded with death pains and death is redemption of that pain which we people often fail to discriminate. "That meaningless word" in the dictionary of Kamala Das is erased for ever as it misguides her from opted path of zenith journey of feminism grounded on pure humanity.

The fifth poem in this series is all about hope and despair playing the game of hide and seek. She in the expectation of good confronts languour and evil, the common play of women's domestic life. "I hide behind my dreams ....../ the winter's mist." She is in the state of confusion not finding capability to bifurcate day from the night. Yet she investigates inside her mind to find "gumption or confront myself" to sort out proper path for further movement that is to "let you down. / They called me winner." Her ultimate aim of life is to stand victorious in the battle of injustice customarily inflicted on women despite endless sacrifices:

> with words I did
> weave a wondorous raiment fit for gods and with
> nimble foot steps climbed the stairways of my
> thoughts
> finding even heaven's portal afar.

It is human society that can be made fit for God to

emulate by purifying our works and thoughts process, maintains Kamala Das. In Hindu scriptures it is well explained that earth is a better place than paradise because one has right to work and think only on earth which is not possible in heaven. John Milton has justified "the way of God to man" in initial section of Paradise Lost. Like a philosopher poet Kamala Das has crossed over the limit of feminism by including topics of universal value in her poetic discourse:

> My songs echoed in stranger's dream, in unease
> they stirred in their sleep and sighed. Yes, often, poets
> gatecrash into the precincts of other dreams
> as Gods and goddesses do many a time
> in unsolicited magnanimity.

Kamala Das for the welfare of woman and society in general has born the mask of God to transmit her gospel of poetry into the ears of strangers who has been reluctant about better half's wellbeing. Her teachings are stirring their mind by contents and most often stay unsolicited like the blessings of divine.

The sixth poem pulls back the author onto old track of feminist debate where she confronts her mutilated self drifting here and there. She is dischanted from the fake love pledges addressed to her by husband. She compares her with a boat bereft of rowers, oars or sail-destination. But blood circulating in the veins of Kamala Das drives her back to original patriarchy where she has emerged from. The familial graveyard of Kamala Das has been turned as a "municipal playground" full of scattered bones and mutilated woman organs over there. The symbol of football ground having children there is indicative of unrestricted liberty Kamala Das is going to avail in future. And, "in the southern wing of ancestral / estate where the coconut trees have nailed down/ the matriarchs bossom with thirsting root." This symbol is a show of confrontation between outgoing patriarchy and setting in green matriarchy spearheaded by

Kamala Das. She has been cheated by in–laws for many times as the following lines show:

> ....not for me the beguiling promise of
> Domestic bliss, the goodnight kiss, the
> Weekly letter that begins with the word dearest,
> Not for me the hollowness of marital
> Vows and the loneliness of a double–bed

Marital bonds, loneliness of double–bed goodnight kiss, weekly letter opening with dearest that Kamala Das was addressed with, has been mere beguile and insubstantial, concludes Kamala Das. Lust of woman is often highlighted by male counterparts as immoral and unethical in comparison to their own. The feminist lust as society has propagated is shrouded in darkness of mystery which does not like to see "another sorrowful day." She would prefer to "lie then in kind night's embrace, soothed by its / blinded compassion ...." The evident distinction between day and night for Kamala Das is working as "anesthetizer of her private sorrow." She would not prefer to awake from night slumber because consciousness of day is dense in darkness, hence it is futile to trip from one darkness to another.

> I shall not
> awake with tearfilled eyes again or look
> down the chasm of another sad day
> to perceive each and every time only
> the debris of the past night's genial dreams.

As a conclusion Kamala Das wants to summarise her life events as repetition of evils one after the another constructing a fragile tower out of debris.

Women's life apparently looking rapturous is bound to sustain on the path of torture and agony as a present of marriage. Inside the mind of tortured woman flows the stream of hemlock that can end her. The eighth poem deals in sorrowful journey of women which she undertakes is "the most torturous" and that carries you "step by weary step." Gradully her pain goes on intensifying and enlarging. Her life is a "general drama of pain" having not even an "interlude of occasional happiness" using the Hardy's phrase, Kamala Das offers the tragic face and bottom of women in the following words:

> beyond the bone and the marrow
> into that invisible abode of pain,
> yes, that deathless
> creation tethered to yourself
> and contently struggling to wrest
> itself free, tethered to your form.........

The relationship of wife to husband in Indian marriage system is inseparable no matter first one's life has become a draught of poison. As the shadow cannot be cut away from the body by any competent surgeon so is wife tethered. Other journey can be cut short or extended a the need arises but matrimonial journey has to continue whatever be the condition of suffering partner.

The last but one poem is an explanation of life which almost every poet has tried to explain. The true meaning of life comes out either in "early youth" or in "weary age" beyond these stages life is meaningless maintains Kamala Das:

> The middle is an opaque
> glass pane, muddied by fingerprints.
> In meaninglessness, trapped, I must
> so remain and taste the outer
> rind of human pain and the seeds
> of mirthless laughter.

The middle age is a period of physical and material enjoyment where understanding of world is the least. Man and woman in youth stay in the state of erotica ignoring undiscovered corners of life that contains finer human qualities like innocence, wisdom and sense of others in the time of sore needs. The last tenth poem is in nut shell of what Kamala Das been battling for all her life to gain. Man's knowledge of life and love is imperfect until one reaches the "red road" that finally ends its patience proverbial." The road is culmination points of worldly experiences turning into wisdom and understanding that help one to adjust well with turmoils of surrounding. The "random caress or the lust / that ends in languor. / its embrace is truth and it erases / even the soul's ancient indentations ...." The journey of life for a man / woman of world is not lust, languor or soul's indentations but fusion of all three. Balanced and working lifestyle can be ascertained from the combination of material, mind, love and spirituality shunning which it will be partial and imperfect. Particularly for woman the worldly life is more challenging as she is pivotal in domestic system expected to be "perfectly structured" to welcome all members of family.

Conclusion

The foregoing study of Kamala Das's entire poetic output is dome with a specific purpose to trace out aesthetic elements emerging form battling feminist life with society, family and surrounding. Every poet offers things which invariably transcends text and context that is correct with Kamala Das too. Most of the poems of Kamala Das are written in "I" that links to author's body, mind and soul. Her experiences are not borrowed or transferred from elsewhere but practically lived on body and mind to collect materials for poetry. She is a poet of feminist longings by the circumstantial forces of which she has been a protagonist. The first chapter, "Veiled Beauty" studies poems written in the period of 1951-60 when Kamala Das was young and energetic youth of twenty five. Her observation of surroundings and the women's interaction as unsatisfied entity has given tremendous issues of poetic composition. No poet, as a matter of fact has been fully accommodated to his time and circumstances. So, Kamala Das too, was in a hot water all her life with her time consequently creating poetry and some fiction mainly on the theme of feminism. The decade of sixty was known for Gandhi-Nehru impact on socio-political and domestic mood of India. Both pioneering leaders of fifties and sixties have dubious view toward liberation of women from the chains of superstitions, illiteracy and obsolete conventionalism.

The chapter makes very well examination of the beauty of women's body and brain that nature has gifted lying so far unused. Neither women nor society is finding any application of that brain and body of half of population, which is proving burden instead. Kamala Das wanted to pierce the veil covering personality and potentiality of women by different methods. In poems like "To a Big Brother (about to be married)", "An introduction", "A Hot Noon at Malabar", "Nani" and "My Grandmother's House" Kamala Das is powerfully vocal against meaningless coverings on the physique and mind of women. She introduced herself to society as a free and individual women wishing to express her poetic longings in the language of her choice. In the matter of familial relationship she respects all but pays no undue importance even to husband. In the game of love she asserts her own sexual requirement equal to that of partner. She prefers that sexuality which is adequately prompted by mutual understanding otherwise it is a kind of personality assassination strongly resisted by the author. Society and family find impetus from mother's and grandmother's compassion barring which it becomes a dictator's house unfit to live in.

The second chapter is "Beauty at War" analyzing poems written during 1961-70. From social point of view this period is known for multi-layered conflict in the life of women against social and traditional confinements. She knows well that centuries old social customs cannot be demolished overnight unless she has a roadmap in hand to offer. The poems under this chapter are full of mythological references to "Radha - Krishna" and "Vrindavan" who served as an ideal love parameter. At the same time she hits hard at man made ethics for women. In "Loud Posters" she strongly recommends "three dimensional nudity" on the pages of monthlies, quarterlies and weeklies. The life of women has been jailed for centuries to examine the strong four walls of husbandial confinement. She admits her to be "Freak" in matters of love, sex and individuality. She casts her glance from domestic women's suffering to dancing eunuchs who are treated by insensate society as puppets. In fact society itself is dead in dealing with women and eunuchs that Kamala Das criticizes. Her opinion that no respectable position women can secure without raising war against injustices. In the long drawn war sometimes she finds frustration yet very soon she restores energy to keep it up as the goal is at hand. Her war against patriarchy is multi-faceted, she attacks relations, family-structure, religion and socio-political practices which are largely responsible for women's subjection in the view of the author. Her strategy of victory provides different opportunities to cull aesthetic points for current age women. Feminist aesthetics must take form by women's struggle maintains the author, not be prepared by gazing male eyes.

The third chapter "Freed Prisoner" is a celebration point in the writing career of Kamala Das spanning from 1971 - 80. The regime of Indira Gandhi as first woman prime minister of India is a dawn of new feminist era where all discordant forces are gradually falling dawn. The womenfolk have felt and projected their intellectual energy in every field of life which were traditionally male dominated. The poems studied in this chapter are sign of festivity entering the freed life of women. They are much ahead of their traditional counterparts in matters of family, society, politics and above all humanity. Despite various opposite pullings women have certified their progress not only for themselves but for society at large. They do not misinterpret the meaning and intention of "freedom" to be identical to lawlessness and exploitative as male has been doing. Freedom in the feminist phraseology contains love, equal opportunity for self and other's existence and identity and creation of a world system based on genuine love.

Kamala Das does not forget to proclaim her specific

identity that cannot genuflect to any unjust authority or institution. This mood of the author is manifest in "Glass" and "A New City". She is mentally and bodily prepared to register her contribution with male participants in dealing with domestic and existential matters with utmost sincerity. In this period her area of observation has considerably enlarged from feminist issue to social, political cultural and most importantly existential. Her pattern of composing poetry is completely unconventional that may be dubbed as prose poetry. Her symbols, images, metaphors and similes are borrowed equally from nature, science, society, religion and mythology. To maintain contemporary tone intact she uses woman's body in a series of poems in a photographic manner but her description is never pornographic. Woman's body as male gaze wants to put forth is not Kamala Das's intention, rather she wants to focus on woman's body as he wishes to underscore their physical value and grace over the male's.

She rotates her early ideas into newer contexts with a desire to show that despite various changes society has not fully accepted women's existence equal to men's. it is a social and psychological phenomenon that takes a lot of time to transform centuries old evil into normal course of life. Kamala Das has tried her hand and luck in various fields of life: from poetry to politics and family to street every where she confronted the tough battle set by patriarchal mind set. The change of society is tough but change of mindset tougher, this fact she knows very well therefore she brings in emotional references to grandmother.

The fourth that is final chapter is all about "Formation of Aesthetic Territory" after going through life of all round turmoils. Kamala Das's concept of beauty is wider and deeper encompassing merits of mind and body. These poems are outcome of 1981–90 a period that is spectacular in feminist affairs overriding masculine domain. Womenfolk have proved their supremacy in every field of life. The family, education economy, administration, defence, science and technology cannot run smoothly shunning the contribution of women in various capacity and position over there. The conservative concept of aesthetics available in Puranic and medieval literature mainly composed for appeasement of royal courts is strongly condemned by Kamala Das for their parochial and filthy approach to women. She pleaded by her poetry the universal capability of feminist mind and physique as an essential part of all system that man has constructed over the years with the development of human civilization. Women's works and contribution in society, love and companion we receive all the time should be taken into account while passing final verdict on them. Vatsyavan's view of woman is narrow, in addition to that she is source of energy, love, motivation, sacrifice, bravery and most intimate counterpart of men without that human life is not possible on earth. The notion of "ardhanareeswar" is well admitted in the proper concept of man - woman relationship. Myth of Radha - Krishna is brought on the plane of post modernity which under the concept of pop - culture and cinema has commodified the existence of women. Women in the writing of Kamala Das are wonderful blend of power prepared by myth, body magic and matter in post modernity where they go for even nudity unhesitatingly to assert their physical and circumstantial value. They at the same time are prompt to fight with any person coming in the way of self-identification. They whole heartedly expose their "bodily hunger" uncaring what would be social reaction. Her logic supporting flamboyant lust is that it is common in male and female, why then women's lust be covered in the mask of shame.

Kamala Das's vision of religion is pacific despite being born in typical south Indian Hindu family she braced Islam perhaps to understand women's position over there. All humanistic qualities of different religions she wanted to inculcate in her personality but orthodox evils she wanted to up root there from. Religion, according to Kamala Das must be a highway of lifestyle not a stagnant pond of violence as in recent times society has witnessed across the world. She has clear cut observation of shrewd political strategies pulling entire world into the furnace of world - war the third time. All regional disputes must be tackled with utmost urgency propelled by common man's welfare and maintenance of humanity at any cost otherwise tiny regional dispute can induce global war. Formation of political parties on the principle of cast, creed, religion, language and ethnicity are same as sowing the seed of poisonous plant that is a must grow in coming future. Among all these issues Kamala Das has very powerfully focused the role of womenfolk in bettering the social system. The trait of spreading love among the people of different origin is specific in women that Kamala Das highlights as main corner stone of feminist aesthetics.

In "Postscript" I studied her poems which are titled "Annamalai Poems" composed in a series of ten poems. From first to last she talks of Annamalai hill as an object of zenith she wanted all her life to ride. The sespentile ways are practical difficulties that Kamala Das or any other woman has to encounter with exceptional zeal because it is created by pallocentric mentality over the centuries. More than victory, Kamala Das values, the strategy and the movement as far as feminist battle is concerned.

Bibliography

A

Alexander. Meena, *Women in Romanticism* (New Delhi: Orientlongman)

B

Balmires. Harry, *A History of Literary Criticism* (New Delhi: Macmillan India)

Basu. N.K. & Sinha. S.N, *Women in Ancient India* (New Delhi: Kamala publishers)

Beauvior. Simone de, *The Second Sex.* (London : Picador 1988)

C

Chindhade. Shirish, *Five Indian English Poets* (New Delhi:Atlantic Pub & Distri . 2001

Cixons. Hiline, *"The Laugh of the Medusa", Contemporary Literary Theory,* ed. (Atkins; 1980)

D

Das. Kamala, *The Best of Kamala Das;* (Kozhikod : Bodhi Publication house, 1991)

________, *My Story*, (New Delhi:Sterling 1976)

________, *Summer in Calcutta* (New Delhi: Orient Longman)

________,*A Dozen Poems* (New Delhi : Orient Longman).

________,*The Old Play House and Other Poems* (New Delhi: Orientlongman)

________,*The Alphabet of Lust* (a novel) (New Delhi: Orient Longman)

Dwivedi. A.N. *Kamala Das and Her Poetry*(New Delhi: Atlantic Publisher & Distributor). 2009.

________,*Papres on Indian Writing in English* Vol - I New Delhi: Atlantic Publisher & Distributors 2001)

________,*Paper on Indian Writing in English*, Vol II. (New Delhi: Atlantic Publisher & Distributors, 2002)

Das. Bijay Kumar, *Post Modern Indian English Literature* (New Delhi: Atlantic Publisher & Distributors, 2003)

F

Freedman. Jane, *Feminism* (New Delhi : Viva Books)

G

Gandhi. Leela, *Post Colonial Theory*, (New Delhi:OUP, 2004)

Gopal. N.R. & Sachar. Suman (eds). *Indian English Poetry and fiction* (New Delhi : Atlantic Pub. & Distri 2000)

Gall. M. Sally, and Rosethal. M.L., *The Modern Poetic Sequence : The Genises of modern Poetry* (N.York : OUP, 1983)

H

Hutcheon. Linda, *The Politics of Postmodernism* (London : Routledge & Francuo Group,2003)

I

Iyengar. K.R.S., *Indian writing in English* (New Delhi: Sterling Publishers, 1983)

Iqbal. Kaur, *"Protest Against Sexual Colonialism* : Kamala Das's *"My Story", "Women's Writing :Text and context"* ed. Jasbir Jain, (New Delhi: Rawat Pub. 1996)

J

Jaidka. Manju, *Recent Trends in women's Poetry,* (New Delhi: Prestige Publication, 2000)

K

Kohli. Devendra, *Virgin Whiteness: Kamala Das's Poetry,* (Calcutta: Writers Workshop Publication)

Kalinikova. Elena J., *Indian English Literature : A Perspective* (Ghaziabad : Vimal Prakashan, 1974)

King. Bruce, *Modern Poetry in English,* (Bombay: OUP, 1987)

M

Molvi. Z.F., *Kamala Das : Homeless in City* (New Delhi: Critical Specturm)

N

Naik. M.K., *Indian English Poetry: From the Beginnings upto 2000,* (New Delhi: Pencraft, 2006)

__________, *Narayan Shyamala A. Indian English Literature: A Critical Survey* (New Delhi: Pencraft, international, 2004)

__________,*A history of Indian English Literature* (New Delhi: Sahitya Academy 1983)

__________, (ed) *Indian Response to Poetry in English* (Madras: Macmillan, 1981)

Nandy. Pritish, *Indian English Poetry Today,* (New Delhi: Sterling. 1975)

Narasimhaiah. C.D. (ed), *Makers of Indian English Literature* (New Delhi : Pencraft International 2003)

P

Piciucco. Paolo Pier & Mittapallis, R., *Kamala Das : A Critical Spectrum* (New Delhi: prestige Books)

Pope. Deborath, *A Separate Vision: Isolation in Contemporary Women's Poetry* (Balon Rogers: Lousiana State 1984)

Prasad. G.J.V., *Continuities in Indian English Poetry: Nation, Language Form,* (New Delhi: Pen craft International, 1999)

R

Raveendran. N.V., *The Aesthetics of Sensuality* (New Delhi: Prestige Publication, 2000).

Roy. Anuradha, *Patterns of Feminist Consciousness in Women Writers,* (New Delhi: Prestige Books 2004)

Reddy. P Bayapa, *Indian Writing in English* (New Delhi: Prestige Books, 1990).

Rahman. Anisur, *Expressive Form in the Poetry of Kamala Das* (New Delhi: Abhinav Pub. 1981)

Radha. K, & Das. Kamala, *Kerala Writers in English Series*: Vol. 8 (Madras: Macmillan, 1986)

R. Parthsarthy, (ed) *Ten Twentieth Century Indian Poets* (New Delhi: OUP, 1984)

S

Singh. Surjeet Meena, *Six Women Poets* (New Delhi: Prestige Books 2003)

__________, *Six Women Poets: A cross Cultural Study,* (New Delhi: prestige Books), 2003.

Seema. Suneel, *Man-Woman Relationship in Indian Fiction,* (New Delhi: Prestige Books, 1995)

Saha. Subhas Chandra, *Modern Indo-Anglian Love Poetry* (Calcutta : Writers workshop, 1971)

Singh. Ram Sewak, & Singh. Charu Sheel. *Spectrum History of Indian Literature in English* (Jallandhar: ABS Publication, 1997)

Z

Zide. Arlene R.k., review of, *The Old Playhouse and Other Poems* by Kamala Das, *Journal of South Asian Literture,* 16 - 1 (1981).

Index

E

U

V